T0043891

PRAISE FOR *PLENTY GOOD ROOM*

"*Plenty Good Room* lays out in clear terms the hope of democratic socialism for a country ravaged by intensifying capitalism. This exciting read is written with such grace, wisdom, and passion, from beginning to end. My generation often wonders what will happen to the world we helped create. *Plenty Good Room* gives an entrée into the future."

—**Andrew J. Young**, former US ambassador to the United Nations and chair of the Andrew J. Young Foundation

"These are apocalyptic times defined by the unrelenting, unsustainable, and unjust reality of growing inequality. In Andrew Wilkes's brilliant new book, Plenty Good Room, he lovingly invites us to imagine and co-create new economies grounded in abundance, in which everyone can thrive. May we all be bold enough to join the movement."

—**Rev. Jen Bailey**, founder of Faith Matters Network and author of To *My Beloveds*

"In *Plenty Good Room*, Andrew Wilkes offers the biblical and theological foundations for economic democracy. Rooting his arguments in Black prophetic religion and principles of democratic socialism, Wilkes demonstrates that there is no distance between Jesus and justice. *Plenty Good Room* preaches the good news that ending poverty is possible. In fact, it's what God requires and what all people of conscience must make real."

—**Rev. Dr. Liz Theoharis**, executive director of the Kairos Center and co-chair of the Poor People's Campaign: A National Call for Moral Revival

"In an era of diminished expectations and political disenchantment, Rev. Andrew Wilkes has produced a call for a socialism that is both moral and democratic. It's the type of work that can reach far beyond the confines of the existing left to a silent majority that yearns for egalitarian solutions in an era of extreme inequality."

—**Bhaskar Sunkara**, president of *The Nation* magazine
and founding editor of *Jacobin*

"*Plenty Good Room* is a call to action, a call to the altar, a call to return to a 'Black social Christianity,' as he calls it, that convicts us and compels us to fight against empire and capitalism. Scripture asks us to 'write the vision, make it plain.' Pastor Wilkes does just that: welcoming community organizers and clergy alike into a politics of abundance, combining a grounded socialist vision with a divine spiritual mission for us all. *Plenty Good Room* is essential reading in these times. The anecdotes, the stories, the teachings from both past and present will leave your cup running over."

—**Phillip Agnew**, co-director of Black Man Build

"With a 'sanctified stubbornness,' holy hope, and fierce faith, pastor and political scientist Andrew Wilkes puts forth an expansive, imaginative, inclusive, and inspiring vision for the possibility of an economic democracy within a beloved community. In resistance to the myth of scarcity, he inscribes the truth about God's abundance in the world through a hospitable spirit in which there is always plenty good room for all flesh. Take and read, and you will be filled with prophetic hope."

—**Rev. Dr. Luke A. Powery**, dean of the Duke University Chapel
and professor of homiletics and African and
African American Studies at Duke Divinity School

PLENTY GOOD ROOM

PLENTY

CO-CREATING AN ECONOMY OF ENOUGH FOR ALL

GOOD

ANDREW WILKES

ROOM

Broadleaf Books

Minneapolis

PLENTY GOOD ROOM
Co-creating an Economy of Enough for All

Copyright © 2024 Andrew Wilkes. Published by Broadleaf Books, an imprint of 1517 Media. All rights reserved. Except for brief quotations in critical articles or reviews, no part of this book may be reproduced in any manner without prior written permission from the publisher. Email copyright@1517. media or write to Permissions, Broadleaf Books, PO Box 1209, Minneapolis, MN 55440-1209.

A portion of Chapter 4 previously appeared as "MLK Rooted His Anti-Capitalism In His Christian Ministry," an essay originally published online at *Sojourners*, sojo.net.

Library of Congress Control Number: 2023947382 (print)

Cover image: © GettyImages-862013794
Cover design: Kimberly Glyder

Print ISBN: 978-1-5064-9151-6
eBook ISBN: 978-1-5064-9152-3

To my brilliant beloved,
Rev. Dr. Gabby Cudjoe-Wilkes

CONTENTS

ACKNOWLEDGMENTS

I have been writing this book, in some ways, for a decade. This now-realized dream, as Scripture maintains, is sweet to the soul. Thank you, first and foremost, to Rev. Dr. Gabby Cudjoe-Wilkes, my wife, partner in ministry, and as Stevie Wonder sings, the sunshine of my life. At every step along the way, your erudition and encouragement have kept me on the path so that I could finish this project. I love you and thank God every day for you.

To my mother and father, Dr. Jettie Burnett and Dr. Shelby Wilkes, for your unwavering support, prayers, and decades-long example of Black Christian witness, service, and community impact. To my brother Martin, for your humor, inspiration, and exemplary commitment to excellence and self-development. To my aunts, Myra and Sonia Burnett, for your love, your gracious acceptance of all my hugs, and your leadership in community, church, and society.

To Rev. Dr. Gwendolyn Long-Cudjoe, for your love and contagious, profound commitment to prayer and communion with God, which has indelibly uplifted my life.

To my sisters in love, Frances and Emily: Frances, for your embodiment of imagination and boundless creativity; Emily, for your warmth, sense of humor, and temerity.

To my brother in love, James, for your modeling of integrity, vibrant faith, consistency, and dedication to family. To Father Selwyn, for our shared love of letters and education as a pathway toward freedom.

To my nephews, William, Josh, Christopher, and Malcolm: May God continue to bless you and undergird your growth in love, purpose, and courage.

To Rev. Dr. Aaron Parker, my pastor, who licensed and ordained me into a Christian ministry and public witness that is "living to love and loving to serve."

To a great cloud of witnesses, through whom I find the strength to run on and see what the end will be: Claudia Vera Jones, W. E. B. Du Bois, Rev. Reverdy Ransom, Rev. Dr. Katie Cannon.

INTRODUCTION

The book you now hold in your hands is an appeal to cocreate the economy that we all deserve, that we all so deeply need. It is part prayer, part call to action. It is not intended to be a blueprint for the future—some fixed, unchanging ideal, springing from spirited but finally unwarranted confidence. It is, rather, an argument for mutual, overlapping action, and for a many-sided movement. It's an invitation to develop the societies that we want for our children, our siblings, our elders, our infirm, our planet.

Here's the reality: modern US capitalism has created a scenario where, as of December 2022, 1 percent of the population, which is predominantly white, holds more of the country's $140 trillion in wealth than the bottom 90 percent of the population. With such a skewed, lopsided, and racialized distribution of asset ownership, democracy is effectively impossible.[1] A popular, potentially apocryphal version of this idea is often attributed to former US Supreme Court Justice Louis Brandeis: "We can either have democracy or great concentration of wealth. But we cannot have both."[2] Millennia before Brandeis expressed that sentiment, Jesus addressed this moral contradiction in similarly stark terms, declaring that we "cannot serve both God and mammon."[3] And his mother Mary, in her prophetic song before his birth, declared that the rich will be sent away empty, the hungry filled with good things; the mighty, pulled down from their thrones.[4]

Building a democracy where working people have a governing say at the workplace, at the ballot box, in society, and within mass media will require, at minimum, having a totally different conversation about money, public finance, and wealth than the one we're having now. Those most responsible for creating our wealth and our way of life—the multiracial population of folks working on farms and in warehouses, office spaces, ports, and homes—deserve substantial agency in setting the terms and rewards of their labor and collective inventiveness. This vision is effectively the polar opposite of how work is currently organized in our country.

Frankly, beloveds, we are in a crisis situation, one that will require the full measure of our moral outrage, vivid faith, and collaborative problem solving. This book is a summons to realize the best of the multiple faith traditions and political perspectives that shape our public life.

Contrary to dominant narratives of austerity, scarcity, and exaggerated cries of resource constraints, there are more excellent ways to tell the story of our economy and to make joint decisions about our common life. Telling better stories and making more equitable decisions demand that we ask a better set of questions. Who gets to live where, and why? Who owns the supply chains upon which we all depend? Whose childhoods are well-resourced, and in what respect? Who gets to enjoy good medical care, affordable housing, living-wage jobs, well-kept parks, well-run mass transportation? Who gets to retire well, and on what terms? Who, exactly, determines the governing principles of production, distribution, and access to public goods that everyone needs but few enjoy?

A recurring line of reasoning in this book is that there is plenty good room for all of God's children to lead fulfilling lives—lives rooted in an intertwined blend of material abundance and cultural enrichment, lives that are meant to be enjoyed as widely, as deeply as possible.

BLACK SOCIAL CHRISTIANITY

The title of this book, *Plenty Good Room*, emerges from a saying in Black churches across the United States: "There's plenty good room for all at the foot of the cross." This proverb expresses an anti-scarcity conviction of Black social Christianity and contends that no one is ineligible for a life of enough, of agency at work and home, of enjoying all the things necessary for a beautiful, fulfilling life. I recognize that *Black social Christianity* may be an unfamiliar term. Here's what I mean by it. Black social Christianity refers to an African-descended tradition of the religion of Jesus that insists on what Alison P. Gise Johnson calls "institutionalized loving-kindness"; prioritizing direct service and civic organizing as an expression of embodying good news to poor communities; and undoing the economic and cultural violence of class domination.[5] The tradition of Black social Christianity, as theological ethicist Gary Dorrien explains, is based on "affirmations of human dignity and divine justice" as well as the "belief in a divine ground of human selfhood" that "powered struggles for black self-determination and campaigns of resistance to white oppression."[6] Black social Christianity names a way of envisioning and performing covenant: of being bound and bonded to persons of faith and goodwill as members seeking to build a beloved community.

We'll use *Black social Christianity*, for the purposes of this book, interchangeably with the term *Black Christian socialism*. Black Christian socialism, which we will look at in more detail in chapter 4, holds that sufficient grace—in its spiritual, economic, and cultural forms—exists for unemployed, underemployed, and undocumented folks; for redlined, over-policed, and abandoned communities; and for the entirety of a beautiful, rapidly warming planet.

Religion is a formative influence that shapes our social and emotional lives, our faith, and ethics. At its best, religion binds the heart of each toward the other, plants our feet on holy ground, and connects all of us to God. At its worst, religion twists our hearts against each other, in words and deeds, and in the process, alienates us from the Divine. In Black Christian socialism, religion concentrates our focus on the very communities to which the day-laboring, peace-bringing Jesus belonged: the dispossessed, the disallowed, the disinherited, the enslaved.

I do not claim that all Christians who love justice must become socialists. But I do maintain that, in a stubbornly unequal world—organized to crush the poor folks toward whom the gospel is directed and whom Saint Paul was eager to remember—all Christians should seriously consider the demand and invitation of socialism.[7] We must analyze the world in deep ways, beyond the slogan-driven, instinctive dismissals of anti-imperial, democratic socialism that pass for analysis in American political culture. We must not limit ourselves to the armchair assessment of white evangelical theologians or moderate politicians committed to the present order.

The universal scope of the plenty good room proverb matters: the intended audience is not a favored few or merely some of us. The "all" of the proverb is not tilted toward investors, executives, and celebrity tech titans who have accumulated financial fortunes under predatory conditions. There's room not just for those of a particular caste, social class, income, religion, geography, or race. Rather, in the words of Grammy award–winning duo OutKast, there's plenty good room for "me and you / your momma and your cousin, too."[8] That is, all of us.

The image here is not barely enough space. It's not the bare minimum of a poverty wage that pays $7.25 an hour, which is the federally mandated wage floor as of May 2023. The image is not of the absurd idea that only some elders deserve to retire with dignity and financial security, while others are consigned to premature caskets due to America's grotesquely underfunded system of social insurance. We can, and should, say no a thousand times over to that vision.

Rather, the vision that imbues this book, and that is rooted in the convictions of innumerable Black churches, is one of plenty good room: ample space for choir practice and recreational basketball leagues; resources for spiritual formation and civic formation; programs dedicated to community and beauty. It is not the will of God—nor even the will of most people—that so many families and households in the United States are merely one crisis, one financial emergency, one sick day away from losing it all.

In a plenty good room society, a federal jobs guarantee and universal basic income would be accessible to individuals as a civil right and as a cushion to inevitable shocks and volatility in the global economy. In such a world, public banks, credit unions, mutual aid funds, and baby bonds would resource the basic needs of families seeking money for a college education, down payment for a home, or an emergency allocation of resources to purchase medicine, groceries, a long-overdue staycation.

A plenty good room society is not a novel idea or recent innovation. Identifying and carrying forward the work of plenty good room is actually a time-honored tradition. It is home-grown, rooted in both the diasporic history of Black people and in American history. It is a historically informed practice of correcting the market failures of our economy at a systemic level through the coordinated efforts of unions, worker centers, community groups, high-road commerce, and the public provision of a *social wage*: a measure that pointedly names the fact that public services and goods are provided not based on charity but based on what human beings inherently deserve.[9]

In an economy in which lopsided trade policies, growth-obsessed macroeconomic decisions, and well-organized interested groups dictate the quality of life for millions, curating a plenty good room society envisions another, more just way.

SANCTIFIED STUBBORNNESS

You hold in your hands a book that I have been writing for the past decade. In these pages I argue that freedom-loving Black folks, as a proxy for all humanity, should consider socialism as a viable political strategy for ameliorating, and daring to eradicate, massive human misery.

As you begin this book, you deserve to know a bit more about who I am. I hold all of my identities together in integration, not compartmentalization: socialist, Baptist-ordained clergyperson, an elder millennial, married, and, as I never tire of saying, Atlanta born. According to conventional wisdom, politics and piety follow environment, and therefore individuals like me should not exist. Atlanta natives who attended prestigious private schools, as I did, are likelier to become champions of Black excellence, Black entrepreneurship, and gradualist approaches to social justice, rather than, say, a pastor, writer, and political scientist who supports a democratic socialism that resists all forms of nation-states dominating other nations and communities. Growing up in Black Atlanta and being immersed in storied Black institutions, such as Jack and Jill and my alma mater, Hampton University, I have retained the best of those experiences while discarding certain assumptions I learned there, such as the idea that misfortune, luck, or merit explains unequal life outcomes in our neighborhoods. I now hold that things like political choices and entrenched forms of injustice—not an individual's work ethic—primarily explain the per capita and standard-of-living outcomes of communities. While developing my understanding of political economy, I gradually understood that it's not misfortune but rather the ill-gotten, tax-sheltered fortunes of the uberwealthy and their appointed stewards that explain inequality. Contrary to what financial literacy coaches often suggest, it is not only at the *household* level but also at the *population* level where government policies and markets intersect and where we must direct our collective attention. At that crossroads of power—the government and the market—decisions are made that largely shape who experiences poverty, to what degree, with substantial implications for life and mortality.[10]

I acknowledge the ironies of who I have become without embarrassment, while joyfully naming the divine grace, community support, individual determination, and the great cloud of witnesses that formed me. Up over my head, as I wrote this book, I felt inspiration from faith-inspired, democratic socialists like Martin Luther King Jr., bell hooks, and Cornel West. I also drew motivation from scholars of womanist social ethicists like Rev. Dr. Katie Geneva Cannon and Rev. Dr. Keri Day. We'll look more closely at the work of some of these leaders in upcoming chapters.

Perhaps you, too, dear reader, come from an environment where the allure of social privilege, a toehold on class power—the squeeze of a hardscrabble upbringing in poverty, or somewhere in between—make your consideration of an equitable economy an unlikely undertaking. And yet, here are we are, joining a long, still-unfolding tradition of persons, networks, and communities who are struggling, inventing, striving, and laboring to cocreate an economy of enough for all.

As a political scientist, I have studied political theory, economic theory, public policy, and democratic socialism. As a pastor, I have delivered eulogies at funerals and buried people who didn't have to die. I have counseled people who should still have their jobs. From my labors in both fields, I have found that democratic socialism, as one current in the larger river of the Black freedom struggle, offers an imperfect yet important way of pursuing justice, loving mercy, and walking humbly with

God. Democratic socialism is an emancipatory practice, one not reducible to any one organization or tendency. I do not claim that such politics are necessary for all Christians to observe; nor do I claim that all politically engaged persons must hold to theism. I'm making a more focused claim: that ordinary people should be able to overrule the reign of wealth, weapons, and industry titans through elections, mutual aid, organized labor, engaged faith communities and movement groups, and the building of a solidarity-driven, non-extractive economy. Instead of being bullied into selling our labor for a paycheck, with limited space for leisure or caring for our families or communities, all of God's people deserve plenty good room.

This book comes from a place of pastoral concern, informed hope, and what you could call "sanctified stubbornness." That's a religious way of saying that I'm convinced that we can craft into being what we haven't yet fully experienced if we dare to do it together. Sanctified stubbornness means a commitment to transforming the impossible into the inevitable. Sanctified stubbornness might be just what we need to figure out and carry out an economy of enough for all.

My hope is that this book is a generous provocation, particularly, but not only, for readers of faith and those who are spiritually inclined. It's meant to provide a counter vision to those who hear entire theories of economic justice built on the slender reeds of Bible verses wrenched from their literary and historical context. Some religious folks invoke passages like, "If you don't work, you don't eat," or "The poor you will always have with you," building their politics and economics on small strands of the Bible while neglecting the great themes of collective liberation, justice for the downtrodden, social reversal, and peace found in that same blessed book.[11] Individual verses, including my own favored verses, are relevant to invoke but inadequate, by themselves, to explain and label our political choices as "biblical," as what "the gospel requires." A more honest, compelling practice is to pair such citations with an explanation of the assumptions and ethical convictions that power our faith, our economic commitments, and our political views.

As alluded to earlier, *Plenty Good Room* pulls from my training as a political scientist whose interests, research, and engaged scholarship have focused on political theory, public theology, and political economy. Political economy is a tradition of investigating the multitiered intersection of markets, governments, and ownership in the production, distribution, and consumption of goods and services. It considers, for example, how the ownership and control of land, real estate, and air rights determines who can live with a roof over their head and who is unhoused. It contends that our economy is not a separate matter to be left to bankers, financial analysts, and stock market traders; on the contrary, our economy concerns all of us. *Plenty Good Room* addresses an urgent issue: how increasing wealth inequality and cultural stigmatizing often translate into ugly forms of political injustice that are justified in soaring moral, economic, and religious language. Overcoming these challenges is possible when we become moral engineers who collectively narrate, design, organize, and pray for the world we inherently deserve.

Most nations other than the United States have encoded not only their citizens' civic and political rights (like voting and freedom of speech), but also their *social* and *economic* rights as human rights worthy of recognition and implementation.[12] Crucially, countries that meaningfully recognize the right to housing, jobs, and food as human rights develop corresponding programs of resource allocation, administration, and support. As of August 2023, the United States had not yet ratified the International Covenant on Economic, Social, and Cultural Rights. Ratifying that covenant would be an important step toward creating a plenty good room society.

Our global economy is not the neutral, level playing field that some people imagine it to be. It is not an equal marketplace of businesses and consumers, buying and selling goods and services on bargaining terms of full information, mutual consent, and relative fairness. We live, move, and have our being not only in God, as the Christian Scripture tells us, but also in a capitalist, racialized, and status-driven world. We all live, move, and have our being in a world where families, communities, and nations eke out their living in the wake of the legacies of transatlantic slavery and colonialism.

Through my doctoral work and more than fifteen years of organizing and advocacy, I have come to understand how many people presume that a liberal democracy—consisting of constitutional guardrails; freedoms of speech, assembly, and religion; and a robust array of civil rights—is sufficient for ensuring economic opportunity and justice for all Americans. Yet the vision of liberal democracy, while alluring, has been both upheld *and* betrayed in every generation and across the generations. In the seventeenth century, the American ideal teetered between democratic experiment and settler colonialism, which enacted ethnic cleansing and the genocide of native peoples. In the eighteenth century, the writing of the Declaration of Independence and the enactment of the US constitution coexisted with the enslavement of African people. In the nineteenth century, abolitionists and a general strike among once-enslaved Black folks ended chattel slavery on paper (though not in fact) and attempted a grand, short-lived experiment in Reconstruction. State governments quickly undermined the seedlings of abolitionist, multiracial democracy, and militias and police forces joined well-capitalized interests to break strikes and discipline labor. Before the century closed, overt white supremacy leveraged state supreme courts and governors' mansions to set the cornerstones of Jim Crow into place.[13] In the twentieth century, then, the labor and civil rights movements won the forty-hour work week, secured time off on weekends, and enacted voting rights, civil rights, and fair housing bills. Yet before the end of the century, voting rights had been sharply curtailed, the FHA and homeowners' loan corporation instituted redlining in predominantly Black neighborhoods, and both persistent child poverty and the stinging pain of mass incarceration continued as modern-day betrayals of free and fair government.

Liberal democracy as an ideal is one thing; practiced hand in hand with racialized capitalism, it is another, far uglier thing. With one ear toward unedited history, the other toward undaunted hope, let us resolve this: the past is not condemned to forever be prologue, nor does the worst of civic inheritance inherently limit the best of what our legacy can be for current and future generations.

In this world, we may do our work with joy, dignity, and not a few stumbles along the way. But many of us do it all with our heads down, our attention mostly given to our loved ones, jobs, neighborhoods, and congregations. That's understandable. This book invites us to look up at our surroundings, at the systems that shape our cultural and material conditions, and to ask how it all came to exist and if there might not be a better way. It asks us to do more than care about an isolated issue of justice here or there and to ask deeper questions; to not only demand but to collectively *live* better answers. Why, for example, is there such an uneven retention of community wealth and power across Black neighborhoods, and how can we change that?

Economics is often "politics in disguise," as the Rev. William Sloane Coffin offered.[14] Economics is also frequently used to sever historically excluded neighborhoods from public investment; to weaponize inflation into a rationale for tolerating rather than preventing unemployment; and to preach financial responsibility and austerity to poor Black, white, and Latinx families in the United States while, year after year, public investment in defense spending continues. Meanwhile, we overlook the moral basis for canceling the material debts that Western, North Atlantic nations imposed on countries in the Global South. At the time of publication, Germany has begun to make reparations to Namibia, but the process needs accelerated implementation, deeper investment, and replication as far as the reach of colonialism and the transatlantic slave trade.[15]

America is an embodied, power-laden debate. The stakes of this conversation about democracy and the economy are coffins, college scholarships, dignity at work and in communities, and the right to collectively bargain. The stakes include the lives of our loved ones and the well-being of our communities. These things that hang in the balance directly shape our material and emotional lives—indeed, whether we will have life itself.

A PLENTY GOOD ROOM MOVEMENT

Finally, this book narrates a bit of my own journey toward Black Christian socialism. Whether your entry point is Blackness, faith, or politics, my prayer is that some aspect of my life story might interweave with your still-being-written narrative. I arrived at a commitment to a reparative, anti-imperial, economic democracy through study, prayer, political organizing among congregations and community-rooted organizations, and examining my experiences working with local, state, and federal governments. Together, those experiences taught me that a love-powered, radical politics insists not only on immediate relief and responsive, equitable institutions, but also demands the impossible of ourselves and the environments that we inhabit. My work is informed by W. E. B. Du Bois, Rev. Addie Wyatt, Ida B. Wells, Rev. Dr. Martin Luther King Jr., and the life stories of other deeply spiritual Black radicals.

This book is a prayerful effort to highlight both barriers to and bright spots within cocreating a world of enough for all. Along the way we will look at what we could think of as "plenty good room moments" in history: times when cooperative economic activity interrupted the normal capitalist way of doing things. Some of these examples emerge from faith communities, such as the mutual aid work of the Free African Society in the eighteenth century and the Mississippi Freedom Farm cooperative in the twentieth century. Some of these plenty good room moments develop in times of disaster. In the wake of Superstorm Sandy, for example, Occupy Sandy, an offshoot of Occupy Wall Street, developed in New York City as a decentralized network that mapped and met neighborhood needs in some of the hardest-hit communities of New York City, following one of the worst natural disasters to hit the Atlantic seaboard in fifty years. In a similar spirit, the pandemic of Covid-19 gave rise to community fridges, mutual aid roundtables, and micro-economies of care and reciprocity. All these things happened within the surrounding context of a crisis of public health and structural, anti-Black racism.

This book, then, is a call to imagine and create a world beyond what bell hooks calls "white supremacist imperialist heteropatriarchal capitalism."[16] That's a mouthful, for sure, but it's also exceedingly precise. Precision is critical in matters of life and death. There are simply too many caskets in some communities and too much hoarded, unearned wealth in the coffers of others.

This book is a call to join a plenty good room movement. It's an invitation to join other folks, organizations, and networks that work for a cooperative commonwealth. There's plenty good room for all of us. And that's plenty good news.

1 | INTERROGATING OUR ORIGINS

Home anchors our identity in the world. Thinking about home involves wading through memories of our origins and the tangled web of emotions about where our flesh-and-blood journeys begin. To use the language of Black feminist icon bell hooks: "We are born and have our being in a place of memory. We chart our lives by everything we remember from the mundane moment to the majestic. We know ourselves through the art and act of remembering."[1] Claiming our memories, including the need to remember them or rearrange them as needed, is a foundational dimension of freedom, psychological agency, and doing right by the rich complexity of our own lives.

Our memories are not value-free containers, some sort of data cloud where we store a record of experiences. Instead, our memories are personal and political. They are a terrain for unearthing, in hooks's words, the "mundane" and the "majestic" moments that shape our lives. Remembering and evaluating our origins is also not simply a personal act; it's a collective retrieval of the past. As we review our immediate family tree, trace our ancestry, or study the history of our people, we surround ourselves with a community past and present.

Examining our childhoods and our early formation, then, is not simply a backward-looking act. Memory is an act of reflection on what we have survived and where we have soared so that, with an eye toward the future, we might weave the best of what we have known into a forward-looking vision. Again, in bell hooks's verdant phrasing, memory can help us make "a world where all people can live fully and well: where everyone can belong."[2]

Everyone comes from somewhere. We all call some place, or some series of places, "here." Even for unhoused persons, those forced to endure migrations, families priced out of their residences, or individuals shamed out of their shelter because of their identities, home remains a social, material experience. Home is something one innately deserves, even if one has never fully enjoyed it. The idea of home as a human right is not an ideal incapable of being realized. Rather, as urban planner Peter Marcuse and sociologist David Madden argue, asserting home as a human right is about "demanding the impossible" as a strategic attempt to both "challenge residential inequality, alienation, oppression, [and] inequality" and to "point towards ways to change" those realities.[3]

Regardless of how and where we enter the world, our own first "here"—our home—becomes the first status quo we've ever known. Home is a spiritual and political category, one that raises the stakes on discussions of affordable housing, rent regulations, and the bedeviling question of who bears the brunt of gentrification costs. Home is about the lengths we will go to ensure that all God's children have a decent, dignified, accessible place to sleep. Home is more than about the costs of renting or buying a place to live in, though it certainly includes those dynamics. Home does not consist primarily in policy trade-offs or some value-neutral process of bargaining between renters and landlords, homeowners and banks. Enjoying home, fundamentally, is about securing expansive, universal, and material conditions of belonging for every individual and family in every neighborhood.

Memory can lead us to interrogate our origins. For some of us, interrogating our origins is the first step toward resisting a politics of scarcity and austerity. The terms of what political theorist Cedric Robinson and American studies scholar Ruth Wilson Gilmore have called "racial capitalism"—industrial market economies that contain an inherently racial practice and racial hierarchy structured into them—have so limited our imaginations that we don't see a route out of that politics of scarcity.[4] Racial capitalism endlessly extends and reinvents itself, not only through economic exploitation but also by reproducing racial anxieties, economic fears, and cultural stereotypes.[5]

Asking questions about where we came from and how that place was structured can help us see the systems that were previously invisible to us. For others, examining our origins is an ongoing practice of *metanoia*. *Metanoia*, which most New Testament translations render as "repentance," is not necessarily a dour word. It's a transformative word, which Jesus uses to inspire critical, careful thinking about our environment in order to reorient how we move through the world.

What might that journey look like for you? What paths might be available if you analyzed closely the circumstances surrounding the city or town in which you grew up or in which you live now? What radical history might you uncover in the places you call home?

Interrogating our origins is a pathway to finding, understanding, and joining plenty good room moments already taking place in our community, region, and context. The purpose of interrogative analysis is not simply to understand how power, oppression, and injustice operate. It is to create a solidarity that can dislodge the tyrannical imperatives of one-dimensional economic growth that dominates our cities, towns, and nation-states. Interrogating our origins is also not an isolated analysis that happens apart from the soil of community. On the contrary, such interrogation happens best when we pose necessary, inconvenient queries—about land dispossession among Native communities, about topics like lynchings, redlining, and institutionalized xenophobia—in the context of community and in face-to-face conversations. As trees need the forest, political education and civic learning thrive in the vibrant, embedded setting of our communities.

RIGHT TO THE CITY

Underlining the idea of home is a political theory called "the right to the city." Geography scholar David Harvey talks about the right to the city as an assertion: that insecurely employed and unhoused individuals deserve to remain in the cities they inhabit and have helped to create.[6] The right to the city includes the ability of everyone, including unhoused or unemployed individuals, to engage in democratic planning and public stewardship of local investment and of public services and programming. Sociologist Anna Domaradzka, following David Harvey, defines the right to city as both "the individual liberty to access urban resources (including space, services and infrastructure) and the ability to exercise a collective power to reshape the processes of urbanization."[7] This right, which applies to suburban, rural, and exurban areas as well, is about creating a sustainable, well-supported experience of home at the household and community level.

Historian Keeanga-Yamahtta Taylor's work helps us understand what the right to the city means by explaining an inverse reality: that the *exclusion* of Black people (through both redlining and unjust housing opportunities on terms that she calls "predatory inclusion") is "absolutely central to constructing, for [the real estate and banking industries], a healthy housing market."[8] In other words, to craft an inclusive sense of home, we have to assess not only the conflict between real-estate capital and a generic vision of working-class people. We also have to examine how distorted forms of socioeconomic *inclusion* like toxic mortgages impact Black folks' effort to enjoy and assert a right to the city in a society of structural racism.

Asserting a right to the city, then, means proactively addressing the legacies of plutocracy and white supremacy so that Black working-class folk—blackness here being a reference to a diasporic people, as well as a synecdoche for all humanity—can meaningfully shape public processes of planning, investment, and resource allocation.

The systemic crushing of the right to the city that we see around us—from Brooklyn to Botswana—concerns me on numerous levels, including a theological one, because it leads to the reproduction of what I call "prayer disparities" across differing communities of faith. Prayer disparities is a term I've coined to name how inequality instills an unequal regime in the interior lives of Black folks, poor white folks, Indigenous folks, and undocumented folks, one that implicitly positions some persons as petitioners and supplicants and other, often affluent, persons as those who effectively function as the vessels to answer those prayers. An example might clarify the image. On one end of the economic spectrum, we have high-net-worth families of faith who may embrace a prosperity gospel, invoking the "prayer of Jabez" from a biblical story in 1 Chronicles 4. They seek a purportedly divine enlarging of their territory and attribute their own wealth and privilege to their hard work and faithfulness to God. On the opposite and more precarious end of things, another family invokes God's protection to hold on to their home, prevent their eviction, and remain in the same neighborhood where their kids go to school or where their seniors access elder care. Prayer disparities names the unjust, uneven experience of race, place, and home across entire populations. This example hints at a dimension of moral injury and community rupture that terms like "housing inequality" cannot quite capture.

The proper response to such prayer disparities and massive housing insecurity is, put simply, to refuse to tolerate them or to accept them as natural. The urge to ameliorate them is better but not sufficient. A more fitting and faithful response is to identify and eliminate them as immediately, comprehensively, and directly as possible.

This goal is impossible under our current system of racialized, neocolonial, and gendered capitalism; in fact, it barely registers as an economic objective. Our economy does not seriously value the right of every individual to be able to have an experience of home—of being able to, in biblical language, sit under their own vine and fig tree, unafraid.[9] Instead, many people in our market-dominated economy regard the consistent, societal gulf between the creation of home and those prevented from enjoying it—due to suppressed wages, landlord denial of Section 8 vouchers, racist zoning policies, and documented bias among bank lenders—as lamentable but unchangeable. Many people see the lack of housing as an unfortunate reality that should be addressed on an individual basis. If you're concerned about housing, we're told, volunteer to help a family find a home; don't ask why they don't have one in the first place.

In the 1980s and 1990s—the formative decades of my upbringing—gentrification and zoning rules displaced economically vulnerable families, and a contracting economy squeezed out many Americans in cities from the experience of enjoying home at prices that they could afford. This incentive-fueled structure of housing development has been named by some close observers as the "nonprofitization" of housing policy, a term that names how governments at all levels withdrew their commitment to house their populations and instead opted to contract that responsibility out to nonprofits, which have fewer resources and less capacity to provide housing opportunities than governments do.[10]

The fundamental question is whether our homes—our countries of origin, the cities or towns of our birth—can create plenty good room for all their residents, students, citizens, and community members. Are our hometowns places of plenty good room for all? Or do our places of origin create positive, livable conditions only for a few?

ATLANTA

Atlanta is my hometown, and it is where I was exposed to the rich, complex traditions of Black social Christianity. In his book *Dancing in the Darkness*, Rev. Dr. Otis Moss III explains how this tradition took shape in Atlanta. Moss walks through the contributions of key faith leaders and scholars within Black social Christianity, including the pastor and pioneering radio presence of William Holmes Borders, the educator and former Morehouse College president Benjamin Elijah Mays, and Rev. Martin Luther King Sr., among others.

Like many of us, I grew up without knowing the radical history of my own city. As T. S. Eliot opined, sometimes we have to travel all the way around the world to come back home for the first time. I had to interrogate the origins of my own city in order to understand what made it work—and for whom it worked and did not work. What I discovered is that Atlanta—like so many of our towns and cities—is at once a beautiful metropolis and a rigidly top-down, unequal culture. It's a place where the wealthy exercise their rule through the power of corporations as well as the reach and authority vested in local government. But it's also a place where radical history unfolds alongside the history of the powerful.

Only after I became an adult would I discover an amazing plenty good room moment in "the A," as Atlantans affectionately call the city. In 1881, twenty Black women who worked as laundresses in the city formed a workers' organization called the Washing Society.[11] As domestic laborers in white people's homes—underpaid, overworked, and in danger of all sorts of sexual and physical and emotional abuse at the hands of their employers—the washerwomen withdrew their labor and went on strike. The Washing Society exemplified effective, class-conscious, gender-conscious coalition-building: growing their ranks from twenty to three thousand workers; partnering with clergy to hold mass meetings; and organizing white laundresses, a fact that observers called "an extraordinary sign of interracial solidarity for the time."[12]

The women built up so much support that they nearly called a general strike, a move that would have brought the entire city of Atlanta to a standstill. As a result of their groundbreaking organization in the shadow of white racial terror, they raised wages for Black women and established not only laundresses but all Black women workers as absolutely "instrumental to the New South's economy."[13]

This important dimension of labor history is not as well-known as, say, the Fair Labor Standards Act of 1938, which established both a minimum wage and the forty-hour maximum work week that created the weekend as we know it. But the reality is that the Black women's Washing Society organized the first women's strike in the entire country. The Washing Society demonstrates the power of Black women who organize for self-determination over their labor, their dignity, and their income.

What is the radical history of your community? What patterns of congregational activism, labor campaigns, and social movement have occurred in your neck of the woods? One critical step toward co-creating the world we deserve is grounding ourselves in the antecedent efforts of our forebears. This meant, in my case, learning about the Washing Society, as well as the Atlanta Student Movement for Human Rights. The latter movement for human rights is a landmark of student organizing in higher education, a movement that birthed the "triple L" movement for love, law, and liberation and baptized people like Julian Bond, Rev. Otis Moss Jr., Dr. Roslyn Pope, and so many others into the Black freedom struggle. That student movement changed the world by writing "An Appeal for Human Rights," one of the most powerful youth-authored statements of justice ever penned. They conducted nonviolent protest and cultivated the courageous, civic capacity of college students. Through grounding myself in the efforts of my ancestors, I learned about the Student Nonviolent Coordinating Committee and the Southern Christian Leadership Conference, both of which located their headquarters in Atlanta.

The German theorist Karl Marx provided great insight that's relevant to our places of origin when he noted that "each of us make our own history but not under circumstances of our choosing."[14] In other words, while we can decide to make a home of our hometowns, we cannot choose the matrix of opportunity, wealth, income, and decision-making power into which we each are born. Only as we get older, as we develop self-consciousness, and as we cultivate an in-depth understanding of the world around us, do we develop the curiosity and confidence to question and shift the distribution of resources and services around us.

In the language of economist Heather McGhee, we begin to look around at our communities and ask, "Why can't we have nice things"?[15] Why can't every neighborhood, particularly in communities where having a backyard isn't possible, have access to a beautiful park? Why not have clean air, excellent water for drinking and bathroom use, and clean soil for farming in every community? And to pose a question that Rev. Dr. Martin Luther King Jr. once asked: Why do we have to pay for water in a world that's two-thirds water?[16] Why do we accept a society that takes necessities from the masses of people to give luxuries to the upper classes? Why do we accept inequality as a badge of realism, or racial capitalism as the best that we can do?

Asking "why," "why not," and "what if" questions is a tool of design thinking. Questions of justice are instruments that shake the status-quo cobwebs from our thinking in order to make the world that our imaginations, our conscience, and the best of faith traditions tells us is possible.

What may appear to be natural, inevitable, and immutable in the places we live—whether they are our hometowns by birth or our adopted hometowns—turn out, upon scrutiny, pressure, and interrogation, to be matters that are changeable. We can begin to interrogate the status quo by participating in a walking tour of political education in our hometowns, or by attending seminars at a local library or university that reviews regional history. Through organized effort—pooling our prayers, our money, our hope, our anger, and our labor—we can rewrite the rules. We can restructure the uneven power relations of society to create a more equitable ecosystem of justice.

SEGREGATiON iN CASCADE HEiGHTS

I was shocked to discover that Cascade Heights, the neighborhood of my birth and one of Black America's most iconic and leafy enclaves, was once a community forcibly closed off to Black families and aspiring Black homeowners. In 1962, Atlanta mayor Ivan Allen erected what was known as "Atlanta's Berlin Wall": a fence on the street designed to prevent the first handful of Black homeowners from integrating the mostly white Peyton Forest neighborhood.[17] Can you imagine that sort of explicit place-based racism? The restriction of mobility due to race is a function of racial capitalism and one of the environmental impacts of what Black power advocates once called internal colonialism. Not only did white Atlanta decide where Black folk would live

27

and work; they also controlled, utterly, the types of loans Black families could obtain and the kind of land and soil upon which Black families could live. That kind of exhaustive control and unchecked say-so of white folks over Black and poor families is textbook institutional racism. It's also an exercise in neocolonial social engineering, in which a ruling class, often white, shapes the life outcomes of another part of the population, often Black, without their consent and at their expense.

Lamentably, the legacy of such neocolonial social engineering is still with us today, across America's neighborhoods, cities, and towns. Housing, as scholars like Peter Marcuse and Steve Madden and Keeanga-Yamahtta Taylor have shown, is where racial capitalism and uneven financial power impacts folks of color, poor folk, returning citizens, undocumented individuals, and unhoused folks hardest.[18] How else can we explain that as of June 2023, households relying on a minimum-wage job cannot afford a two-bedroom apartment virtually anywhere in the country?[19] How else can we explain the fact that unhoused families sleep under bridges when vacant housing and underutilized office towers in many downtown areas could be converted into cooperative housing, high-quality shelters, and public housing communities? We made public investments in housing following World War II. Why can't we do it now?

We all have an Atlanta, in the sense of a place-based origin story: a hometown where we enter the world. That point of entrance for me is the centerpiece of what was then called the Dirty South.[20] Coming to terms with Atlanta put me on a path that would lead me to self-identify as a democratic socialist, pastor, contemplative, writer, and human being trying to lead a decent, spirit-filled, and impactful life.

PARABLE OF RACiAL PARADOX

Atlanta, it turns out, is the only major metropolitan area in the country that has been run by Black mayors, successively and without interruption, since its first Black mayor assumed the leadership post. Maynard Holbrook Jackson took office in 1974, as the fifty-fourth mayor, and Atlanta has had Black mayors ever since. Jackson was elected just two years after the National Black Political Convention took place in Gary, Indiana. It was a time of optimism, stemming from the first generation of Black mayors assuming office in major cities, as well as a time of frustration, with the unfulfilled promises of freedom and an economy that would deliver a high quality of life for Black families.

One of the lessons of my hometown is that Black political leadership, while important, is not a guarantee of effective, just administration in local government. On the one hand, Atlanta expanded job opportunities for minority and women-owned business enterprises, built a world-class airport, and positioned itself as a globally influential city. These accomplishments notwithstanding, the city also tore down its public housing and implemented zero-tolerance, tough-on-crime policing that helped lay the groundwork for mass incarceration.

Atlanta, then, becomes a parable of racial paradox for how people who have been historically hated as deviant can preside over and even intensify regimes of racial inequality, harsh policing, massive housing insecurity, and hollowed-out structures of employment opportunity. Journalist Teresa Wiltz notes in *Politico* that Atlanta is both a "dynamic, ever-growing . . . hip-hop capital . . . while also being the 'capital of racial disparities,' " a place where "Black entertainment moguls live in gated suburban compounds, while others in impoverished pockets of Black Atlanta struggle to get by."[21]

Starkly put, Atlanta illustrates that laws with racially disparate impact can be designed, marketed, and administered by people who aren't white men. For all its many virtues, my beloved Atlanta also demonstrates that systems of capitalism and authoritarian government can be maintained even when individual officeholders are increasingly diverse by race, family background, gender identity, country of origin, ability, and other facets of identity. In other words, it's possible to achieve inclusion and diversity among mayors—even governors and presidents—without redistributing decision-making power, wealth, opportunity, and agency in a transformative way.

My experience of Atlanta taught me that othering and scapegoating poor people, Black people, neurodivergent people, and anyone we paint as different and deficient is, regrettably, an American practice. When I was ten or eleven, I graduated from Romar Academy, a predominantly Black private elementary school, and enrolled in Woodward Academy, a mostly white private institution for middle and high school students. As a child, I intermittently thought about what the gulf, and connection, between those social worlds meant. Going from my largely Black neighborhood of Cascade Heights to the enclosed setting of Woodward taught me a great deal. Sometimes I'd notice the difference in the built environment between traditional public schools and that of my school; the contrasting appearance of the athletic facilities, libraries, and performing arts centers made those distinctions especially apparent.

I also noticed that the informal circles of the Black managerial-professional class—where the children of lawyers, doctors, and accountants would meet—offered ready-made explanations for those differences. Some adults insisted that whatever distinctions existed were negligible. They maintained that individual factors of student achievement and teacher preparedness mattered most: not resource allocation, not greater investment of money and technical assistance, not better facilities. A handful of adults assigned political factors to those distinctions, pointing out that students in lower-income neighborhoods accessed fewer high-quality learning opportunities than those in higher-income ones. These conversations filled out the curriculum that I did not receive at my predominantly white school. Within church basements, the living rooms of family friends, and the carpooled rides to and from sports practice, those discussions about how different Atlantans experienced our shared home taught me, over time, about the value of sustained, critical thinking about place, race, and belonging.

At Hampton University in Virginia, my first opportunity to build a "home away from home"—indeed, the school's motto is "Our Home by the Sea"—I began to pair sustained, critical thinking with the values of community service. At Hampton I learned, in an experiential way, that everyone did not grow up in a single-family home, as I had. While I knew that already, the reality of wealth stratifications and vastly different life outcomes within Black communities began to click in a new way. At Hampton, I started to wonder what makes a home and why some people had less access to it. Walking around campus by the Chesapeake Bay, I eventually learned that public policy, laws, and social norms—not personal choice or impersonal fate—crystallized residential apartheid into the maps of not only my hometown but hometowns across America, across the world. That understanding went deeper over time, but it first took root at a historically Black college and university.

Our initial experiences of home offer us a theological and political curriculum. With the support of outside resources and by engaging in community, we can function as both student and teacher in this curriculum. We might learn, for example, that lamenting the blend of white supremacy and socioeconomic inequality every February for Black History Month—and perhaps now, every Juneteenth—while also refusing to implement the structural measures needed to level inequality partly explains our inability, or worse our lack of desire, to make change.

For example, I grew up hearing that "an ounce of prevention is worth a pound of cure." Yet I recall little discussion among my peers or adults about how to demand that the local government resource, market, and scale up "prevention" programs in institutionally disinvested neighborhoods. It was as if much of Black Atlanta had withdrawn its political clout from the community problem-solving work of self-determination and left impoverished siblings to struggle on their own, civically abandoned, and, effectively, politically alone.

The blunt truth is that my two private school experiences in Atlanta both provided a stellar liberal arts education and, seen together, served as finishing schools in white supremacist culture. At such schools, one learns how white-dominant culture often cloaks cutting judgments in humor, and how awkward cross-cultural exchanges about dress, food, and music reveal bias against minoritized peoples. Examining my own experiences of racial difference in Atlanta's private schools taught me that schools always teach multiple curricula—the instructional materials in class and the unofficial lessons learned about racial identity and inequality. It was a significant step toward constructively interrogating my origins.

The questions of my home, of Atlanta, are the questions of all our homes. What stories explain the different outcomes of children who attend elite schools versus those who attend more modestly resourced ones? How do political leaders, local news companies, and the economy reinforce and reproduce the worst edges of racial capitalism? What hopeful attempts to ameliorate, redesign, or (gasp) transition away from that system into a solidarity economy are occurring?

These questions are not for show, nor for political theater. They are, instead, deliberative and hopefully constructive questions meant to urge moral engineering: tearing down outdated stories, false myths, and anti-Black, anti-Indigenous ideals that dehumanize all of us and frustrate the emergence of a more ethical humanity.

THE REWARDS OF INTERROGATING OUR ORIGINS

Interrogating our origins can be difficult work, but it is also deeply rewarding. Such thoroughgoing inquiry is what led the people of Evanston, Illinois, to embark on a reparations program. Evanston became the first city in the United States to initiate a plan of reparations for the descendants of enslaved African Americans. In 2020, Evanston decided, as the first phase of a multistage process, to allocate $25,000 grants to sixteen residents.[22] That public choice marked an imperfect yet courageous start to a long-overdue project. As an analogue to the plight of Black people, it is worth noting that America issued reparations to Japanese families who suffered forcible tenure in internment camps during World War II.

Questioning the built environment and narratives of home—rather than avoiding, romanticizing, or merely critiquing home as a concept—can lead us to a multidimensional appreciation of our heritage, a sense of tradition, and the inspiration to co-create an economy that works for all. For me, learning to identify the hierarchal relationships of power in our society led me to a blunt truth: the palatial estates that some wealthy people call home are dependent upon the insecurity of other families.[23] In my home neighborhood, Cascade Heights, I saw this preventable injustice up close and personal. During the Great Recession that began in 2007, elderly people in southwest Atlanta were steered into mortgages with incomplete information that concealed ballooning terms. Economic injury to families in Atlanta did not occur within a vacuum, but rather within a broader economic shock of America's system of racial capitalism. Consequently, families in formerly segregated neighborhoods in southwest Atlanta saw vacancy rates hit 43 percent. That's merely one snapshot of a larger picture of financial ruin that, in the aggregate, cut residential wealth among Black families nearly in half.[24]

When we parse through the starting points of our origins, we can discover, as the residents and citizens of Evanston did, the collective opportunities and benefits for repair and redressing the inherited harms of our past so that we can build a more equitable future.

EVERYONE DESERVES A PLACE CALLED HOME

Let's return to the right to the city. If you read local newspapers across the country, you could be forgiven for thinking that only politicians, political parties, CEOs of major corporations, and their lobbyists have a right to the city, the town, the suburb. This is also true of well-heeled nonprofits, whose professionalized operations sometimes present their own institutional priorities as if they were necessarily the issues of primary concern for their stakeholders. Take Covid-19 relief funding as an example. During the pandemic, the Trump and Biden administrations authorized unprecedented amounts of funding to be used to stabilize business, local nonprofits, and all manner of organizations. That injection of support, so the story went, was targeted to the most needy, most community-rooted of institutions. Corporations like Shake Shack and other wealthy businesses indicated that their receipt of Covid-19 funds was not truly needed, returned the funding, and noted that propping up their organization was effectively beyond the scope of legislative intent for the disaster funding.[25]

Such reactions may appear to be publicity stunts, but they are better understood as dramatizing design flaws in our social policy. When the communities hardest hit by a once-in-a-century illness do not have a straightforward process for their residents to meaningfully engage with the federal policies designed to help them, those residents' and citizens' right to the city—or town or municipality—is undermined. Even in 2023, as this book goes to press, the racially and economically disparate impacts of the pandemic remain. We face a rollback in eviction moratoriums and decreased efforts to combat mass incarceration at precisely the time when we most need to double down on those efforts.

Corporate involvement, far too frequently, holds the decisive say on a whole host of issues: from the priorities of economic development, to zoning laws, to public transit plans, to the decision about whether a stadium or a flagship branch of a college will be constructed. Once such decisions are set, they are then— to the chagrin of few in power and to the frustration of most residents—marketed as opportunities for "community input." The result, too frequently, is that local planning and land use policies figuratively (and sometimes literally) take our homes from underneath our feet, while the mechanisms for *participating* in the design process are effectively restricted to elected officials, lobbyists, and government agency staff.

Here I am thinking of how zoning that prioritizes sprawling, high-rise condos can overhaul traditional landscapes in neighborhoods without community members being offered sufficient information or opportunities to provide input that meaningfully influences the final decision. These sort of faux community input processes occur under the conceit that private owners are entitled to dispose of or sell their land without any sort of social claim. In direct contradiction to this prevailing mythos, Pope Francis argued that there is a social claim on all private property. Pope Francis's idea, here, is that the enclosure of land for individual use is not an absolute good but rather a conditional one. It's something that makes social sense only insofar as it benefits communities. The good of families and individuals retains an inviolable importance, but one that must often be subordinated to a higher common good discerned through public, informed debate.

Cities and local communities committed to plenty good room—that is, committed to a sense of providing home and belonging for everyone—invest in the full continuum of housing rather than over-investing in ownership strategies. When cities assign exaggerated importance to property ownership, in pursuit of what former President George W. Bush once called an "ownership society," they prevent the needs of renters, commercial tenants, and industrial leaseholders from being fairly and justly represented. They obscure the asset-cultivation strategy of communities through parks, public banks, credit unions, and community land trusts. We should insist on political representation at the institutional, programmatic, elected, and constitutional level—representation that better enables all residents and citizens to both make and preserve a sense of home: rented, owned, or otherwise experienced.

Cities and local communities, instead of becoming ownership societies, can invest in a full continuum of housing options in order to become a beautiful quilt of inclusion for all residents. Such strategies and guarantees might include land-use planning and zoning that prioritizes investments in public housing, supportive and transitional housing, affordable rental housing, affordable homeownership, and shelter housing. When that housing is paired with a public health strategy that makes medicine accessible, preventive care attainable, and supportive services within reach: well, then we've moved a bit closer toward plenty good room for all.

PLENTY GOOD ROOM IN THE CITY

The first protest I ever attended was a rally organized by the Concerned Black Clergy of Atlanta. I must have been around twelve, though time has removed my clear recollection. What I do remember is a deep sense of the value of community members engaging in justice work.

We met in the parking lot of the neighborhood supermarket down the street from my childhood home. Again, I don't remember the exact reason for the protest, but I know the late Rev. Dr. Barbara King, founder and pastor of the Hillside

International Chapel and Truth Center, delivered riveting remarks. That day also impressed upon me the principle of co-creation: clergy and lay people gathering to amplify a cause deemed important to everyone assembled. Whatever the issue was, they recognized that it was too difficult for them to move alone, solve alone, protest alone. Only in a community—only as a gathered group—could they move the needle and achieve lasting change.

Creating plenty good room boils down to moments like the protest in that parking lot. Plenty good room moments are times in which anger is assembled rather than atomized. They are the times in which individuals' desire for change coalesces into a coalition. Ensuring that our hometowns and places of origin create—and preserve—plenty good room takes more than individual agitation; it takes concerted, continual, and collective labor. To create plenty good room for all, we need to cultivate the know-how and the passion to project our power, across electoral cycles, business cycles, and seasonal cycles, in small groups and large ones.

And once assembled, we stay together. We stay together until paid sick leave passes in the legislature, until foreclosures are prevented, until worker coops are within reach of every community. If we organize long enough, we can stop economic policy from implementing corporate giveaways that are mislabeled as business attraction strategies; indeed, we can, if we so determine, advocate for local and statewide agencies that build genuine social enterprise, workforce housing, and public healthcare. Coming together and staying together, identifying not only isolated issues but common causes of inequality: this is how plenty good room moments come into being.

Every hometown, not only my own of Atlanta, contains a circle of faith and community leaders who hold on to a vision of plenty good room. When such leaders join with neighborhood activists, university centers, unions, and other community-based networks, we can bring a plenty good room society closer to reality. This vision prioritizes the abundant life that Jesus promised as more than an ahistorical, abstract vision of Christian doctrine. Rather, it is a vision that contains anti-scarcity convictions of "God's gratuitous love"—in the language of Peruvian priest and liberation theologian Gustavo Gutierrez—that underwrite concern for both one's own family and the kinship of all humanity.[26]

My personal introduction to the plenty good room tradition of Black social Christianity began with my early exposure to labor unions that provided college scholarships for book expenses. It began with the feeling of plentitude I and others experienced in serving slow-cooked meals to unhoused individuals and families—with plates and plates to spare—in downtown Atlanta. It began with constant exposure to the legacy of the civil rights movement intersecting with, and to a large degree, emerging from Black Protestant churches in the US South. Growing up in that setting, it was as if the enjoyment and exercise of civil rights—of freedom of speech, of religion, and of assembly—were basic and fundamental to the mission and activity of God's faith communities in the world.

WHAT DOES WELCOME LOOK LiKE?

Communities can dedicate funding, talent, and prayer to being either welcoming or unwelcoming. What do unwelcoming local communities look like? They invest in boondoggle plans of stadiums and condos as economic development strategies, promising exaggerated job creation numbers that rarely materialize at the scale predicted or on the timeline upon which they are marketed. Unwelcoming communities rely on chambers of commerce, business improvement districts, and banking conglomerates to be the senior partners of commerce, with labor unions, worker centers, and research institutions as the junior partners. Communities invested in plenty good room, by contrast, work in the opposite direction: giving credit unions, public banks, and publicly controlled sovereign wealth funds equal standing—even the lead roles—in innovation.

Democratic socialisms—for there are a variety of them, wherever the term is invoked with a sense of tradition and substance—aspire to create hometowns, town squares, and public venues that are truly welcoming to all residents, community members, and citizens. Welcome, here, does not merely mean attitudes of tolerance, forbearance, and polite, uniform acceptance. Such attitudes do not contain the genuine virtue of welcome but are instead only semblances of it, and sometimes full of condescension and paternalism. True welcome means that ethnic studies courses, mental health supports, and LGBTQ clubs in schools are not viewed as a departure from academic rigor but rather essential educational priorities that deserve robust funding. Authentic welcome means inviting voters into political community by making it easier to know how, when, and where to vote at community centers, public concerts, congregations, and college campuses. Welcome also means co-creating the public goods, social ownership, and equality of decision-making power that makes sufficiency and "enoughness" a reality for prenatal care and for maternal health options.

True welcome invites individuals into the economy not only as consumers but as workers, equitable entrepreneurs, and planners. Genuine welcome, the kind that creates a durable sense of home, equips all persons and families with expertise that suits their passion, skills to operationalize that passion, and a vision to contribute to a cause bigger than themselves. Authentic welcome invites individuals to understand themselves as artists, as enjoyers of art, and as just human beings. When that interconnected sense of welcome is supplied, then our cities, rural areas, and towns will be true sanctuaries of welcome. To the extent that these things happen, we will have truly welcoming hometowns. Until then, welcome has not reached its fullest, most important meaning.

Creating welcoming cities and towns means more than hosting cross-cultural dialogues or sensitivity trainings on implicit bias. Welcoming communities, as the students of the Atlanta Student Movement saw, use the power of love and the resource of law in the public square toward liberation. Together we can begin to undo American apartheid. That lesson is as true for us now as it was for them then.

Interrogating our origins is a political and spiritual practice that can build empathy, connection across lines of difference, and the willingness to work together to dismantle an economic culture and system that no longer works. It is not simply our policies that need redesigning. We *ourselves* need renovation: how we remember home, how we carry the past with us as a point of reference, how we take responsibility for our neighbors.

2 | JOINING AN UNDERGROUND RIVER OF FREEDOM DREAMS

Life intends—which is to say, God insists—that freedom be our birthright. All of us, not just a favored few, deserve the beautiful and the good. I think of our longings for freedom as an underground river: a current of desire streaming toward the full emancipation of ourselves, of our planet, of Black peoples, and our economies. That river of laughter and liberation may be covered up in ads and algorithms, but it remains. It remains, with a holy stubbornness, all the same. Flowing within us, like a creek forever determined to rise, is a freedom dream.

My mother's generation of college students had a freedom dream. Together they started Black studies programs across the country. First, they dreamed of a better, more inclusive curriculum—one that ensured that African American research, history, and theoretical contributions were taught to students. Then they sprang into collective action.

In 1968, Mom and her student colleagues took over the Main Hall on the campus of Vassar College, one of the historic "seven sisters" colleges of New England. For days on end, they slept in that building at the center of the campus. They received food from the community, made memories and commitments to each other, and placed their burgeoning careers and young adult comforts on the line. In a lengthy protest calling faculty and administration to account for ignoring Black contributions to disciplines across the academy, they put enough pressure on to effect real change. As a result of their protest, Vassar College students now enjoy an Africana Studies program that recently celebrated its fiftieth year.

I attended that fiftieth anniversary celebration with my mother, Dr. Jettie Burnett, and my wife, Rev. Dr. Gabby Cudjoe-Wilkes. There, while walking around with my mother on the grounds she once traversed, we learned the power of a freedom dream. We discovered that she, too, harbored an underground river of freedom—a vision of Black students like herself enjoying an educational experience that took their community, history, experiences, and distinctive research interests seriously.

What informed that work and joint effort? My mother and her classmates worked successfully to make real their vision of an open university, one truly affirming of Black student presence, not just in name or on paper only. Mom's example of student activism alongside her peers, her example of community service and healing in medicine, and her theological legacy of church instruction are gifts that she handed to me. From Mom, I learned that outrage can translate into thoughtful, collaborative action, and that such action can make a pivotal difference in the life of our institutions.

Mom embodied freedom dreams for me before I ever encountered that idea, which we'll look at in more depth in this chapter, in a book by historian Robin D. G. Kelley. She taught me that individual achievement, however praiseworthy, is insufficient as the primary goal of human labor. I also learned from her that disruption alone is inadequate. Pushing back against status-quo arrangements of power must go hand in hand with recreating institutions and networks to serve the common good. Uprooting the current arrangements of power and business as usual is commendable; even better is dreaming and designing a different, more just society. In this case, my mom and her fellow students who occupied the Main Hall at the university not only "stuck it to the system," so to speak; they also successfully applied pressure for a more complete, more African-centered education for Black students. And that's a curriculum that—surprise, surprise!—benefits all students curious enough to pursue a well-rounded education.

Scrubbing away what white supremacy and racial capitalism stamp on our spirits takes work. It requires emotional and social support. It entails a reconstructed arrangement of authority and learning that works not only for students but for all faculty, administrators, and community stakeholders. A young, soon-to-be Dr. Jettie Marita Burnett co-led a charge to reorganize how history and liberal arts education was understood. Mom's story is part of a larger, generational story of learning justice and reinventing academic institutions. Countless student visionaries, on their own campuses, helped to start the Black studies movement and thus instituted access to Black studies and Africana studies for succeeding generations.[1]

That shared vision—creating something for forthcoming generations to inherit—*that* is the unglamorous, holy work of realizing freedom dreams. Making these kinds of dreams real entails carrying on ancestral legacy and family inheritance. In that sense, freedom dreams connect us to the past and the future.

What are your freedom dreams, beloveds? If freedom is indeed a constant struggle, as the scholar-activist Angela Davis maintains, what kind of labor or shared undertaking might God be calling you to undertake?

Before we look more at freedom dreams, let's consider a notion I like to call confrontational contemplation, which I believe goes hand in hand with freedom dreams.

CONFRONTATIONAL CONTEMPLATION

Contemplation means abiding in the space between what is and what could be. Contemplation places us between what Rabbi Abraham Joshua Heschel called "radical amazement" and what political writer Bhaskar Sunkara calls "the class struggle of social democracy."[2] Conventionally painted as an individual withdrawal from society to connect with the Divine—the sort of practice that happens in monasteries, retreat centers, and labyrinth walks—contemplation can lead us to apprehend the world with wonder, awe, and sustained gratitude. This is the dimension that Heschel calls radical amazement.

Rev. Dr. Barbara Holmes, a womanist mystic, contends that contemplation is a "spiritual practice that has the potential to heal, instruct, and connect us to the source of our being."[3] Contemplation, at its best, is a practice that can heal us while connecting us to the creative Caregiver. We need the kind of contemplation that connects us, like an underground river hidden within our imagination and intuition, to the One of whom the psalmist says: "be still and know that I am God."[4]

But alongside the awe-driven, wonder-filled consideration of what is, contemplation has a *confrontational* dimension as well. This aspect of contemplation is what led Rabbi Heschel to march in Selma, Alabama, against Jim Crow apartheid and America's anti-Black rejection of fully representative democracy. Heschel famously referred to this type of contemplation as "praying with your feet."[5] This dimension of contemplation, in many respects, is what led Dr. Holmes to work as an attorney, scholar, and political biographer of the late Rep. Barbara Jordan.

Confrontational contemplation is the link between Moses's mystical moment at the burning bush and the "let my people go" challenge he issued to the Pharoah. Confrontational contemplation is what NAACP members did when they marched in deliberate silence down Fifth Avenue in July 1917 to protest lynching and racial terror. It's what enslaved people did in the rapturous singing of "We Shall Overcome," an anthem first lifted up in the fields of the southern United States, and it's what workers in Charleston did later, in 1945, when they intoned the same song in strikes against the American Tobacco Company for better pay. It's what protesters did in the civil rights movement of the 1960s, when they sang it as a freedom song.[6]

Confrontational contemplation is the devotional practice of exposing social evil, engaging in community problem-solving, and undertaking the work of class struggle in order to build a truly beautiful society in which bounty is shared by everyone. At first glance, it may seem odd to pair contemplation with the Marxist idea of class struggle, which envisions a virtually perpetual conflict between the *interests of workers*, who produce most of the financial value in the supply chain of organizations, and *the interests of owners and investors*, who unjustly capture most of that value through wage scales, tax codes, and monetary policies skewed in their favor. Yet the connection becomes clearer if we remember that our struggle is not against flesh and blood but against what one ancient writer called "principalities," "powers," and "spiritual wickedness in high places."[7]

We become motivated to join class struggle not by individual antipathy for the uber-rich, nor envy their gilded lives. Class struggle is, instead, about opposition to systems of capital accumulation and profit maximization in supposed democracies that exalt the preferences of the rich over the human rights and dignity of the most vulnerable. Class struggle is a sacred rejection of state-sponsored, corporation-backed attempts to enclose and privatize God's creation for a tiny club of humanity. Class struggle is also a shared striving by working people to co-create organizations, public goods, and social wealth to ensure our own survival and to uplift our collective quality of life.

If *conventional* contemplation establishes in us a sense of wonder, awe, and kinship with other people, planet, and plants, *confrontational* contemplation builds on that feeling of interconnectedness. But how, exactly—and why—does confrontational contemplation build on that work? First, the conflictual dimension of contemplation engages in politics, social enterprise, unions, regional planning work, and movement organizations to ensure that the surplus and plentitude of God's creation is as widely and deeply enjoyed as the Divine intends it to be. Second, confrontational contemplation wagers the big-picture judgment that a democratic socialism comes closer to God's beloved community than is possible even for a purportedly "humane capitalism." (Humane capitalism, after all, is still racial capitalism, the latter being a system built on and continuously benefiting from exploitation, colonialism, and the imperial extraction scheme of large countries fleecing smaller, formerly colonized nations for their commodities and labor.)

Jean-Jacques Rousseau, one of the early social contract theorists, offers a cue that forms the beginning of a response to the question of how confrontational contemplation might build on conventional practices of contemplation. In slightly paraphrased language, Rousseau once opined: "human beings are born free—yet everywhere are in chains."[8] Pairing Rousseau and Holmes, we can say that human life, as we experience it today, is suspended between an encaging, carceral dimension of society and the potential to be healed, grounded, and free. Confrontational contemplation, in some ways, provides the wellspring of energy that waters our freedom dreams.

AS AMERiCAN AS SWEET POTATO PiE

Freedom dreams require inspiration from and retrieval of traditions, actions, and frameworks of the past. But to be viable, those dreams must find an appropriate form in our current moment. What do the words of freedom sound like when articulated in your own voice and sentences? What aspects of *un*freedom most evoke your ire, your desire to commit yourself again and again to the work of liberation?

Freedom Dreams: Recovering the Black Radical Imagination is a book by UCLA historian Robin D. G. Kelley. Writing in the early 2000s, during the administration of President George W. Bush, Kelley articulated the importance of dreams, visions, fantasy, and futurism within movements for liberation. This chapter's name derives from Kelley's book, which achieves a difficult balancing act: providing historical context for the "long" civil rights movement, labor movements, and early formations for reparations for Black folks, along with a summons to chart a more equitable future than the one that we have inherited.

Kelley's *Freedom Dreams* conveys a basic point that merits repeating in every generation: our imaginations are the source of beautiful art and poetic meaning and also catalysts for resistance and a transformed society. Kelley's insights detail how our imaginations are countercultural and counterintuitive. In today's politics, convening a focus group, commissioning a poll of likely voters, or conducting exit polls of voters are widely perceived as the most valid way to influence opinion on public policy issues. And there is value to be gleaned from defining how the public feels about a given policy issue, to be sure. Yet there is also value to infusing hope and imaginatively projecting what can be accomplished through collective action, divine grace, and historical circumstance.

Freedom dreams, as Kelley reminds us, are not an indulgence or luxury. They are a spiritually grounded refusal to let the bounds of the empirical dictate what is doable, reasonable, or viable. This is an idea, of course, that has a corresponding expression in Scripture. The book of Proverbs declares, for instance, that without a vision, the people perish. What is vision if not a dream: one that illumines our capacity to both perceive the world in its current arrangement and to see the latent possibilities for a more just one?

Freedom dreams can take a multitude of forms. Such dreaming may mean resisting a high school guidance counselor's projection of what career paths are best suited for "someone from your background." Such dreaming might entail resisting the construction of yet another high-rise office tower and instead insisting on a public park or mixed-use property for industrial and cultural use. Freedom dreams could, and often do involve, deliberately rejecting one set of faux dreams in the name of a higher, broader set of dreams.

Freedom dreams stand out in stark contrast to the "American dream" as many define it. A standard dream of liberal democracy, for instance, is a world of inequality made tolerable through the provision of equal educational opportunity from preschool, K–12, college, and potentially graduate school for those who choose that route. Some will succeed, some will fail, this dream suggests, but all will get the opportunity to try. While not terribly equitable, it's a decent enough dream. But why should the scope and circumference of freedom dreams stop at the borderlines of the schoolhouse? We know that both individuals with PhDs and those with only high-school degrees face an unjustly organized economy. Our economy, it bears repeating, is not permanently destined to cluster wealth in the mutual funds and interest-bearing accounts of the wealthy, while the workers who made that wealth possible can't feed their kids. It is the task of dreamers to imagine and to create a society based on abundance, beginning in whatever environments in which we find ourselves.

Kelley also offers an important rejoinder to the idea that anti-capitalism is foreign to American life. Many people think that democratic socialism has no roots in American political culture. They think that anti-capitalist thinking is an exotic import, unfamiliar to Black communities. But Kelley shows that democratic socialism, the push for reparations, and varieties of Black nationalism are all part of a homegrown, sweet-potato-pie tradition, deeply rooted in our public life and history.

The underground river of freedom dreams, and the democratic socialism that it feeds, is a tradition long recognized in the United States. It recognizes that reparation is a policy idea with an ethical rationale to repair historical wrongs, and that working-class communities must exercise decision-making power over the terms of their work, their time, their bodies, their labor. Democratic socialism, in practice (though not necessarily named that way by its practitioners) is a tradition as American as the Southern Tenant Farmers' Union organizing agricultural workers. It's as storied as Charles and Shirley Sherrod, veterans of the Student Nonviolent Coordinating Committee, establishing America's first community land trust near Americus, Georgia. We see freedom dreams in Peter Clark, who is frequently called America's first Black socialist and who served working people in the Midwest region of the country.[9] And in Rev. George Washington Woodbey, whose life and work Philip Foner explores in his seminal text, *Black Socialist Preacher*, a Black Baptist preacher who served congregations faithfully and also worked within the Socialist Party. He pushed nationalized railroads and infrastructure as a pathway to instill racial justice and economic equity in America's industrial democracy. These leaders and organizations, among others, show us that democratic socialism is nothing new or scary. It is, simply, a neglected stream of deeply Black, deeply American, and yet internationalist practice.

The sooner we recognize that democratic socialism is a homegrown American tradition—not an import from another time or place—the better.

HOW DOES iT FEEL TO BE FREE?

The late music artist Nina Simone once inquired, "How does it feel to be free?"[10] Her piercing inquiry remains poignant in a nation that incarcerates a higher percentage of its citizens and residents than any other industrialized nation on earth. Indeed, as both Michelle Alexander's *The New Jim Crow* and the Equal Justice Initiative remind us, America's carceral structure supplies the most direct line from the social order of the plantation, sharecropping, and convict leasing to our current regimes of mass incarceration. Understanding the afterlives of slavery and anti-blackness helps us to understand the racially disparate use of the death penalty and the coercion of incarcerated individuals in states like California into fighting fires and constructing public goods.[11]

Nina Simone's song speaks a healing, invigorating word to us on today. Indeed, her very life still speaks. Through songs like "Young, Gifted, and Black," she extolled the capacity of Black children to develop their divinely endowed potential into careers, vocations, and callings of their choosing and of God's sending. Through songs like "Mississippi Goddamn" and "Backlash Blues," she lyrically and courageously addressed the unfreedom of America. The former song lamented how white Americans exhibited violent angst in relation to the Civil Rights era's cross-generational attempts to dismantle Jim Crow, undo *de jure* segregation, and realize an integrated society. The lyrics alone were powerful enough; the freedom dream dimension, however, is especially evident in that Simone used the familiar format of a Broadway show tune to communicate a difficult truth about the ugliness of racism, political domination, and economic apartheid in the United States, particularly in the Deep South. The latter song depicted white racial fears, as institutionalized by the Ku Klux Klan, the White Citizen's Council, and southern governors like George Wallace and Lester Maddox. Truly, the Civil Rights movement aimed to reconstruct and instill a *second* founding of the country.[12] This necessary, holy, and freeing work may have made a lot of white people nervous, but it also helped a lot of Black people to experience freedom, with powerful ripple effects in migrant labor organizing and the American Indian movement.

Simone's music reminds us that the underground river of freedom often engages the arts, the humanities, and popular culture to sustain the currents of freedom. Music, murals, and the musings of faith traditions are the underground river of freedom in repose, like still waters. Legislation, litigation, coalition meetings, and organizing drives are the underground river of freedom rushing like whitewater rapids. Both versions of the river are needed.

In *Freedom Dreams,* Kelley also addresses how poetry and the surreal—how the stuff of dreams—contribute to our freedom. Art and poetry and music are important on their own terms and as correctives to a vulgar materialism that reduces reality and meaning to a narrow, supposedly neutral set of facts and data. In Black churches across America, this point is driven home by preaching about the difference between facts and the truth. When we reduce material reality to observable facts alone, we unfairly devalue the world of symbols and stories that we find in congregations and in sacred texts like the Bible as well as in street murals, open mic poetry slams, and sidewalk candles that honor the dead.

The resonant lyrics of the prophet Joel also supply content for our freedom dreams: "In the last days, I will pour out my Spirit. Your old men will dream dreams and your young women will see visions."[13] Within the deep currents of the human spirit, the rain of God's own Spirit pours an irrepressible yearning for emancipation.

Like Nina Simone, the prophet Joel prompts us to wonder: How might our prayers and deepest aspirations inspire our dreaming of new visions, our singing of new songs of freedom and radical inequality? Dreaming of liberation isn't reserved for a select few, like politicians and college professors. Everyone can join the work of moral engineering to redesign, re-narrate, and restructure our economy to work for all of us. Civic awakening— visioning for freedom—is a collective epiphany. It's for all of us.

Let's consider a few freedom dreams in history.

INSTANCES OF FREEDOM DREAMS

History, as ever, is replete with examples of freedom dreaming. The Free African Society (FAS) in Philadelphia, founded in 1787, was a plenty good room moment if there ever was one. Led by pioneers like Richard Allen and Absalom Jones, The Free African Society provided support to families needing burials, assistance during illness, and similar services to address their unmet needs, in addition to championing abolition. Their undertaking of mutual aid, in its historical context, is both an example of incredible innovation and solidarity and an indictment of entrenched white supremacy. Of critical note, the African Methodist Episcopal church grew out of the FAS, carrying forward the legacy of abolition, mutual aid, and the universal kinship of humanity, guided by the parenthood of God.[14]

Indeed, in eighteenth-century Philadelphia, the invention of such a society was not only a great idea but a necessary one. Picture the stakes and the depth of moral contradiction: in 1787, the US Constitution was signed in Independence Hall, in precisely the same city where the Free African Society was founded. Allen,

Jones, and their peers had to express Black self-determination through an organization like the Free African Society, because the Constitution was drafted not to promote their welfare but to exploit them for regional advantage, through the three-fifth clause designed to boost the representation of Southern slave-holding states. Nevertheless, defying all odds, the courageous venture of the Free African Society helped to birth the African Methodist Episcopal Church. That denomination has provided decades of spiritual direction, Christian witness, and political empowerment to Black lives. Beginning in the antebellum era and into Reconstruction, a range of institutional Black church denominations—such as the National Baptist Convention, the Christian Methodist Church, and the genesis of what would become the Church of God in Christ—took formal shape. The Black church helped to birth multiple legislative careers, such as the career of the first Black US Senator, Sen. Hiram Revels, and helped form the public witness of socialists like Rev. Reverdy Ransom, who became editor of the AME *Church Review*, and the Right Reverend Theodore Holly Bishop of Haiti.

Freedom dreams gain meaning and content in relation to their environment. Within the early days of America's democratic experiment, freedom dreams meant, above all else, an immediate, comprehensive abolition of chattel slavery, but also, as Gayraud Wilmore has illustrated, an intertwined emphasis on liberation, elevation, and survival.[15] Wilmore's threefold framework is an example of the confrontational contemplation we discussed earlier. Wilmore argued that antebellum piety sought to make life more beautifully and decently human, a vision of utility and aesthetic taste that epitomizes what contemplation calls us to realize. Today's freedom dreams should draw inspiration from the eighteenth and nineteenth centuries, while also painting visions of emancipation informed by our current context, by what Scripture names as "this present evil age."[16]

FROM THE AMERICAN DREAM TO FREEDOM DREAMS

What forces have impaired your ability to compose and conduct what Kelley calls freedom dreams? What is stopping us, collectively, from imagining and implementing? The insistent, consistent visioning toward the world we deserve and desire is hard to unearth without admitting that, as one Black church song puts it: "This is a mean old world, and we have to stay here until we die." True enough. But inhabiting a mean world doesn't have to stop us from making that world a bit more beautiful, a bit more fair.

Pivoting from the acceptance of one dream—such as conventional statements of the American dream—to crafting authentic, sustainable freedom dreams is hard work. But how we interpret our personal experiences can make the difference in whether we lean into the Black freedom struggle or lean out. The lens we apply to make sense of our lives can influence whether we advance a cross-cutting, emancipatory project of joy and justice, on the one hand, or an issue-based campaign devoid of holistic context and long-term impact, on the other. The sweet spot for all of us is to identify the Venn diagram where our passion and personalities overlap with the pressing needs of the world. That region is the interior space from which we can work sustainably and gladly for a world befitting the glory of God and the inherent dignity of both planet and people.

Perhaps you are transitioning from school into your chosen career. It might be that you are considering how your major or minor in college, or how your chosen focus or study in community college or trade school, can lead to an expanded enjoyment of freedom for both yourself and for those who are most crushed by our economy. Selecting a vocation might mean dedicating your talent to improving the adverse socioeconomic conditions facing immigrant workers, incarcerated workers, differently abled folks, Indigenous folks, and on some level, everyone in our society. Professions that could advance the foregoing goals include but are not limited to, serving as a public interest attorney, a community organizer, a healthcare professional, a social entrepreneur with a movement focus. Whatever the setting or occupation, we can commit to ameliorating and abolishing the social causes of our personal suffering and pain. We can fully step into freedom dreams of justice work and the spiritual renewal that such work involves.

By organizing and supporting the increased growth and impact of unions and worker centers, we can advance our own and others' freedom dreams. By serving locally and by coalescing our communities within our neighborhoods—through venues like a political clubhouse, a county-level commission, or a community board—we can walk a bit further into the arena of freedom dreams. What I have in mind here is not becoming an unreflective, passionate participant in capitalist politics that specialize in inequality management. Some activists devote themselves to incremental, "just enough" issues: just enough of a hike in the minimum wage to avoid backlash, but not enough that people can actually live without economic fear.

Just enough affordable housing units to prevent a project from being stalled, but not enough units and certainly not affordable enough to house families in decency, dignity, and the beauty that all families deserve. Freedom dreams are roomier—and more demanding—than that.

FROM HOOP DREAMS TO FREEDOM DREAMS

Like many young Black boys, I found basketball to be a safe, freeing place to dream. The basketball court is where we worked out early childhood dreams of self-actualization, where we learned collaboration and creativity in the spirit of play, and where we tasted a sense of accomplishment and affirmation from our community—even if we lost a particular game. For me, basketball represented more than athletics but functioned as a powerful arena of both self-cultivation and community cultivation.

Despite bringing modest talent to the court, I learned how to work in small groups to realize deeply felt objectives—winning a game, holding our own as the JV team against the varsity squad—as well as the dignity of battling against long odds and the soul-deep satisfaction of staying in the arena for a worthy fight without a guaranteed outcome. Somewhere in between practicing jump shots and layups, somewhere in between running offense and mounting a spirited defense against an opposing team, we discovered that simply being in the fight is important. Along with St. Paul, we deemed it important to fight a good fight, keep the proverbial faith, and finish the race.[17]

Such early experiences are not stages beyond which we grow. We do physically, of course, but not necessarily in a psychological or spiritual sense. Our childhoods—that stretch of time and place where we first exercise our imaginations—can help inspire our work for a more emancipated future for humanity. Whether we are eighteen, twenty-eight, or eighty-eight, the virtue of a spiritual childhood, as Peruvian priest and liberation theologian Gustavo Gutierrez puts it, lies in "opening up" to God and "living in community."[18] Lessons we learned when we were young can help us fight to preserve breathable air on a planet in existential peril, to resist the cynicism of cheap slogans and low aspiration in our politics, and to redesign the infrastructure, guarantees, and incentives of our economy.

Looking back, I find that playing basketball taught me how to adopt an athletic commitment to the life of the mind, to striving for justice, to keeping score of what truly matters. Sports presents one avenue to realizing freedom dreams. In concrete terms, one thinks of the Atlanta Dream WNBA team protesting for voting rights, or the human rights advocacy of NBA legend Kareem Abdul-Jabbar, Bill Russell, and iconic prizefighter Muhammad Ali. Ultimately, for me, carryover lessons from sports taught me the kind of disposition needed to monitor things like passing legislation, keeping track of what's repealed, and forging coalitions to create the conditions for allocating resources, opportunity, and public goods to institutionally underserved communities. Playing basketball, in part, prepared me for training others and being trained in faith-based community organizing. It informed my work as I stepped fully into my calling of writing sermons, authoring books, drafting campaign plans, raising funds, and leading departments and organizations—all the while participating in other networks to advance the work of doing justice, loving mercy, and walking humbly with God.

A ViSiON BOARD FOR PLENTY GOOD ROOM

You could think of a freedom dream as an enhanced version of a vision board. Vision boards are composed of quotations, pictures, and symbols arranged together on a posterboard. In many communities across America—including Black communities and churches—people create vision boards each January to symbolize a future life that they intend to enjoy. When created in community, vision boards can be visual synonyms for everything from new year's resolutions to snapshots of a world without mass incarceration and predatory economies. Each vision board offers glimpses of a life made more meaningful on an intimate, personal level. Vision boards—and any kind of vision casting, for that matter—can be the stuff of prayer, signifying what we hope God will do and what we ourselves intend to do.

Vision boards often stop, however, at the perimeter of the individual person. Vision boards that only imagine personal elevation reinforce individualism. This kind of exercise can tap into self-centered streams of our culture and drain the sacred, underground river of freedom. What does it profit us to excel at executing our individual visions when the larger vision of our communities is frustrated by forces beyond our communities' control? Have we succeeded in making our ancestors proud—whatever our lineage may be—when the scope of our gaze is limited to the flourishing of our immediate family and not our neighbors? Or to our immediate neighbors but not to residents in the rest of our town, city, or suburb?

Responsible vision-casting ties our own future to that of our counterparts in different nations, different faith traditions, different gender identities, and different socioeconomic classes. The goal of such a plenty good room vision is to organize the society we inhabit to more closely resemble the luminous ideals of equality, justice, and solidarity—ideals that the dominant political parties constantly invoke, yet constantly betray. Here's my take-home point: we need a vision with an uplifting, liberating perspective that brings *all* humanity, not just ourselves, into the focus. Otherwise, we will end up spiritualizing selfishness.

Vision casting could be about daring to first-draft and second-draft our way into a freedom dream. We might dream of the betterment of all humanity and the conclusion of oppression. Vision casting certainly is intrinsic to a faithful attempt to follow the Jesus who pledged to set captives free, to preach good news to the poor, to prioritize mercy, faithfulness, and justice, and to interpret every religious idea through the dual prism of loving God and loving your neighbor. For people of faith and moral courage, a freedom dream is an actionable obligation that, by some strange outworking of providence in community, supplies its own inspiration and joy, its own method of nursing our grief and helping us repair what social evils have ruptured. Freedom dreams keep us going until that day when each of us makes our transition from cradle to casket to crown in glory.

At their best, vision boards can be an important exercise in tethering the personal passion of who we yearn to be, as individuals, to a collective hunger of who we might become, together. They can connect our care for ourselves to our work in local congregations, internationalist political organizations, labor unions, neighborhood charities, and associations seeking to tilt the world toward justice. Inspired by Habakkuk, one of the biblical prophets of ancient Israel, we can "write the vision and make it plain."[19] Freedom dreams are the hook upon which our individual visions can be sustainably held, made morally defensible, and rendered theologically responsible.

FROM EACH OF US, FOR ALL OF US

Systemic change is an aspect of freedom work. To pursue freedom dreams capable of confronting social ills—including depression-level unemployment among teenagers of color, effective exclusion from preventive healthcare for too many Americans, and countless other endemic challenges—we need effort, exertion, and a willingness to experiment. Frederick Douglass, the silver-tongued abolitionist, statesman, and Christian of the nineteenth century, once remarked: "The whole history of the progress of human liberty shows that all concessions yet made to her august claims have been born of earnest struggle. The conflict has been exciting, agitating, all-absorbing, and for the time being, putting all other tumults to silence. It must do this or it does nothing. If there is no struggle there is no progress."[20]

Douglass's inspiring words challenge us to see that the "august claims" of human liberty will require us to engage in struggle, agitation, and dedicated effort. It's possible to read these words as a counsel of despair. I wouldn't argue with that interpretation. A better reading, though—one truer to the arc of Douglass's persistent prodding for freedom—is to interpret these words as an encouragement to translate dreams of freedom into the resolution to labor for their fruition.

In the twenty-first century, workers' self-organizing for union representation, such as Starbucks baristas, Amazon factory workers, and airline flight attendants, embody the continuing wisdom and relevance of Douglass's words.[21] No less inspiring are the transit workers in London, pushing back against the economic pressures worsened by Brexit, organizing to ensure better working conditions for their fellow employees.[22] They, too, are legatees of Douglass's counsel to exert ourselves in order to fulfill our freedom dreams. Alongside those notable examples of liberating work are the everyday instances like the Green Worker Cooperatives in the Bronx: a social enterprise and collective committed to gender and racial equity. They have provided coaching and skills training to cooperatives in industries as varied as manufacturing and design to fashion and farming. Those everyday examples are also freedom work to make our dreams a reality.

THE PROMISE OF LIBERTY AND JUSTICE

Within our hearts, where we find the underground river of freedom, we know that we can do better than racial capitalism. We can, and we must. The longing for something other than racial capitalism is an intuition substantiated by the provocative binary of Jesus: you cannot serve God and mammon.[23]

We cannot guarantee the arrival or success of a utopia in advance. But this we know: the sickness unto death that is capitalism will assuredly bury our freedom dreams in a thousand graveyards. I know this to be the case, for I have prepared eulogies and participated in funerals for people whose medical examiner's reports could read as if bell hooks had written the cause of death: white supremacist, heteropatriarchal, imperialist capitalism. The consequences of not moving toward an economic democracy or democratic socialism are not confined to winning or losing a cocktail hour debate; the stakes are whether we move toward a life of thriving or toward one of social misery and preventable deaths.

You may not yet be convinced of the merits of the argument so far. Fair enough. But might we at least fail in a better direction, toward the sunlit promise of liberty and justice for all? I'm wagering—as are so many—that the answer is *yes*. And if it be true that fortune belongs to the bold, then I say to the children of Martin and Malcolm, the children of Ella and Fannie Lou, that a sun-kissed socialism, one in which all persons can derive warmth, might just be the way forward.

3 | REPAIRING OUR DEMOCRACY

Presidential democracies like the United States have a ritual. Every four years, politicians hit the campaign trail in search of votes. They build out advertising campaigns, personnel, and a full-court press to register more voters and then to move those voters to the polls. Within every four-year cycle lies a tighter two-year cycle, whereby voters are asked to vote during a mid-term cycle for members of Congress. If the voting process is representative, goes the standard storyline of political theory, then the consent of the governed has been secured. In other words, we can credibly say that the electorate put our officials in office. If, however, representative democracy is bought and sold by the wealthy and the powerful, undermined by voter suppression, and distorted by massive disinformation about candidates and the policies they stand for, then we can say with the great psalmist Beyonce: America has a problem.

During both of the decision-making rituals that we call elections—the four-year cycle and the two-year one—individual selection of politicians bumps up against a range of factors. There's the design of the Electoral College, a political compromise from the slaveholding era of our republic that apportions votes for president based on the number of US Senators and members of the House of Representatives in each state instead of on the actual population of each state.[1] The net result is a gross distortion of political voice, with a densely populated state like California receiving less representation than Wyoming, a far less populated state. The challenges with such a system are legion. Suffice to say it's hard to encourage voters to retain confidence in the outcome when the process is patently, procedurally unfair.

In a system of racial capitalism, a representative democracy is always at risk of slipping into little more than the buying and selling of influence, rather than reflecting the will of voters. We can sharpen this point a bit more. The settler-colonial past of our nation set in motion a tremendously stubborn fiction: the notion that we can build a representative democracy on top of stolen land and stolen labor, all the while denying full political voice to those populations. That we can strip-mine, extract, and industrialize the earth with no consequences or negligible ones, ignoring the fact that climate change means that our precious earth is casting its own ballot against our way of doing things. That corporations deserve to be able to act more freely than people can, and that the rich somehow deserve to be able to decisively shape the life chances of the poor.

The lopsided impact of the wealthy on our elections illustrates the need for a clear turnaround in order to make the principle of one person, one vote, a meaningful ideal. Heather McGhee, the former president of the think tank Demos and the author of *The Sum of Us: What Racism Costs Everyone and How We Can Prosper Together*, sets forth a powerful case for why and how our politics became so unreflective of its population. On this point, McGhee writes, "Over the past few decades, a series of money-in-politics lawsuits, including Citizens United, have overturned anticorruption protections, making it possible for a wealthy individual to give more than $3.5 million to a party and its candidates in an election cycle, for corporations and unions to spend unlimited sums to get candidates elected or defeated, and for secret money to sway elections."[2]

The structural flaws in our democracy, which McGhee so precisely articulates, pose a serious challenge to civic ideals such as the rule of law, equal justice under the law, and rule by consent of the governed. When wealthy donors—instead of a multiracial, cross-generational, class-diverse electorate—pick our lawmakers, the net result is a rigged system. That system may claim to be carrying out the mandate of all voters, but in reality, as one political scientist once put it, it speaks with an "upper class accent."[3] If the authority of the government cannot be meaningfully traced back to the will of the least wealthy, least well-connected voters, the odds are high that plutocracy—a governance by the uber-wealthy—has eclipsed democracy.

McGhee's indictment of our federal political system is worth noting here again. "The big-money campaign finance system is like so much of modern-day structural racism," she writes: "it harms people of color disproportionately but doesn't spare non-wealthy white people; it may be hard to assign racist intent, but it's easy to find the racist impacts."[4]

As the national electorate becomes diverse, with wealth inequality widening, ensuring the freedom and fairness of our voting process, during both primary and general election seasons, is a moral imperative. And it's too important to leave solely to political scientists, professional lobbyists, and consultants. It's up to each of us, voting for the candidates and issues of our choosing, to cast our ballots in a way that builds enough political power to implement policies that improve the common good of the most dispossessed and the most vulnerable.

In a local or state election, that might mean casting a strategic ballot for a third-party candidate. In federal elections, it might mean voting for mainstream candidates—and under the right conditions, third-party candidates—and urging them to move in the direction of plenty good room through practices like lobbying, shaping the narrative in the press, and cultivating enough power among movement organizations to win critical victories in terms of de-commodified, or free, access to public goods.

As soon as a democratically achieved majoritarian basis can be established—and with the goal of helping to create that majority—we should work toward larger, longer-term goals that move us toward plenty good room. These goals include deeper unionization across industries, which is correlated with higher wages for workers and more regulation of our financial system through a greater proportion of credit unions and public banks. Additionally, we can seek higher community or public control over resources like regional planning of building construction and economic development authorities. This is a great way to protect families from the manifold injuries of racial capitalism while working to build a better, fairer system.

Our democracy is both resilient and deeply in need of repair. To realize the promise of a socialism rooted in civil liberties, economic justice, and racial equity, we must restructure our politics to be more reflective of its people. In this chapter we'll look at several ways by which we might repair our democracy. But first, let's consider in a bit more depth the form of democracy that we have now.

REPRESENTATIVE DEMOCRACY

Much of political theory is dedicated to answering a version of this question: why does one segment of society permit another segment of the same population to rule over it? For most of humanity's long, winding career, the answer has been plain: God appointed this person—or this family, or this social class—to rule. The divine right of kings, queens, and families to command and control the masses has been justified by belief in a higher power who decreed that it be so. Other responses have included the charisma of an individual, the forcefulness of a clan or tribe, or a leader's effectiveness, real or perceived, within a bureau-cracy. The sociologist Max Weber maintained that authority in societies derives from charismatic, traditional, and rational-legal authority.[5] The first lodges authority within special individuals, filled with charisma and force of personality. The second locates it within political myths and religious orders. The last source of authority, which Weber regarded as the highest, most sophisti-cated authority, places the right to rule among a system of laws.

Representative democracy can be a beautiful, hard-won thing. The franchise in the United States was established through struggle, protest, cajoling, parades, civil wars, and constitutional amendments. Establishing the voting rights of women and formerly enslaved African Americans and Indigenous people and others represent a vast, collaborative achievement of justice.

Further, representative democracy is a clear improvement over the divine right of individual rulers to make decisions for entire populations. Across the centuries and depicted in the sacred anthologies of Scripture, we see the presentation of polit-ical authority in the ancient near East and during the Roman

Empire. During that time, political authority generally rested in kings, governors, and emperors: male leaders who claimed a divine mandate to assemble standing armies, conduct a census, or execute a scheme of taxation. Despite the patriarchal, male-dominated society within which the Bible was written, Queen Vashti, the Queen of Sheba, the daughters of Zelophehad, and judges like Deborah demonstrated the subversive grace of God, flowing through women's leadership as a stream of counter-vailing authority.

So far, so good. Representative democracy is a good thing—provided that the principle is maximized, again and again, to the edges of society. Who, for example, effectively represents the needs of the sick for full, comprehensive healthcare? Where is the constituency invested in undocumented individuals and families, making citizenship status and its attendant benefits of labor protections, Medicaid, social security, and all the rest, a reality?

Representative democracy, it turns out, is only as good as those who do the representing. Democracy requires effective, capable representatives *and* inclusive, just conditions of representation. As long as the average amount of money spent on congressional seats exceeds more than $16 million for a US Senate seat and $2 million for a US House seat (thereby sharply constraining who can run effectively for office), and as long as the electorate suffers from electoral misinformation and voter disenfranchisement, "representative democracy" will mean that government reflects the will of the well-connected, well-resourced, and well-educated.[6]

Representative democracy alone does not supply enough power, deep participation, or moral legitimacy to create a plenty good room society. Let's turn now to the promise of three less widely discussed yet essential traditions of democracy: partici-patory, reparative, and economic democracy. If pursued with courage, risk-taking, and the kind of prayer that expresses itself through embodied action, these traditions of democracies can create space for a plenty good room society to emerge.

PARTICIPATORY DEMOCRACY

Participatory democracy—what I think of as co-governance—is an antidote to representative democracy's ills. The shift from representative democracy toward participatory democracy means a change from viewing government as "something they do over there," with our occasional input at the ballot box, to seeing governance as something that all of us do together: before, during, after, *and* independent of elections.

Participatory democracy, in large part, is the language and ethos of social movements. The Civil Rights movement, aboli-tionist movements, the Indigenous water rights movement, the ecumenical movement within churches, and interfaith move-ments, each in their own way, have invoked such language. Election-only participation in the decision-making of society occurs too infrequently; elections are simply too few and far between to actually constitute governance. Resource allocation, programming, and policy-making decisions that benefit society—beginning with working-class people, Black people, Indigenous communities, incarcerated folk, and the most vulnerable among us—require more from us as neighbors, as citizens, as members of an interconnected global community.

Participatory democracy is a flexible concept. Sometimes it means participation *with* government, where congregations and community-based institutions organize job fairs, lead violence-interruption programs, or sign up to be Covid-19 testing and vaccination sites. Such partnerships between communities and governments are critical for the well-being of people—particularly if governments are to be servants for the good of the people, as voices as varied as St Paul in Romans 13 and Rev. Dr. Martin Luther King Jr. have maintained.

Other times, participatory democracy means participation *in* government. Here, one thinks of teacher union presidents running for mayor, pastors serving on local town councils, mothers and aunties serving on school boards and with pillars of civic engagement like the NAACP and League of Women Voters. The work of participatory governance happens both within the system and also alongside—and therefore outside—our traditional systems.

Within the system, groups like the Participatory Budgeting Project model the creation of plenty good room. Let's look briefly at what participatory budgeting is and how it exemplifies an *inside*-the-system approach to participatory democracy. We'll look then at an *outside*-the-system approach, as well as ask what an *against*-the-system approach might be.

PARTiCiPATORY BUDGETiNG

Participatory budgeting, which began in Porto Alegre, Brazil in 1989, fosters civic involvement by assigning a portion of funding that residents can directly allocate to projects and local problems in their communities. Studies indicate that individuals who engage the process increase their civic participation, becoming 7 percent more likely to vote.[7] Participatory budgeting garnered attention worldwide for its inventive method of involving residents, nontraditional voters, and alienated voters in the process of resource allocation and public investment. Eventually, in 2009, twenty years after the emergence of the policy, participatory budgeting hit the United States, first in Chicago and then in New York City.[8]

On a congregational level, I have witnessed the power of participatory budgeting to revive a feeling of personal effectiveness and trust in government. In 2012, I organized a conference workshop on "the people's budgeting," as some advocates called it, at my local church. We invited a staff person from the Participatory Budgeting Project to join a circle of faith-rooted organizers to explain the process, field questions, and urge both church and community members to take part in the work.

The discussion went smoothly enough, but there was no identifiable sign that it had struck a chord. Some months later, one of the parishioners who attended the workshop told me that she not only took the information but used it to engage the participatory budgeting process happening in her local city council district. After she finished that process, she told me how proud she was to have been involved with assigning money for project-based purposes rather than simply volunteering her time—as important as that is—to areas needing development in her community.

A SOLiDARiTY ECONOMY

The New Economy Coalition (NEC) is an example of an *outside*-the-system approach to building participatory democracy. The NEC is a membership-based collective of 200 organizations working to "support a just transition from an extractive to a regenerative economy by building the scale and power of the solidarity economy movement in Black, Indigenous, and working-class communities in every region of the United States."[9]

For background and context, the International Labour Organization defines the *solidarity economy* as follows: "The Social and Solidarity Economy (SSE) encompasses enterprises, organizations and other entities that are engaged in economic, social, and environmental activities to serve the collective and/or general interest, which are based on the principles of voluntary cooperation and mutual aid, democratic and/or participatory governance, autonomy and independence, and the primacy of people and social purpose over capital in the distribution and use of surpluses and/or profits as well as assets."[10] In other words, the solidarity economy is about dethroning capital, wealth, and political power clustered in the hands of a few so that a democracy run by the people can have a chance.

To be sure, members of NEC work with the public sector. But they place the center of gravity on building *regional economies*: place-based ecosystems capable of transcending the political boundaries of state lines. NEC also provides a centralized network of relationship cultivation, information sharing, and power building for cooperatives, small businesses, and nonprofit organizations that are rooted in local communities and deep ownership for collective decision-making. Within these locally and regionally held relationships, their bargaining power is strengthened by and flows from close-knit organization. NEC's work demonstrates that the idea that socialism is somehow opposed to commerce or running an equitable business is a misconception. Democratic socialism does not oppose the operation and management of all forms of private enterprise; rather, it opposes the ownership and management of businesses that exploit employees and prevent workplace democracy, hoard information at the top, and maximize profit at the expense of environmental stewardship, community coalition, and the advancement of human rights.

So far, so good. But what exactly *is* the solidarity economy? The labor movement often frames solidarity as the shared commitment to workers striking for better wages or improved working conditions. In other contexts, solidarity is a call to build multi-issue, multiracial coalitions in which members pledge their expertise, relationships, and resources to realize justice and end oppression.

The solidarity economy carries these connotations and also pushes the conversation further. NEC defines a solidarity economy as "an environment in which all of the things a community needs—like housing, schools, farms and food production, local governance, art and culture, healthcare, and transportation—are controlled and governed by the people, led by those most marginalized by our current economy, and building strong community roots."[11]

Building a solidarity economy means crafting a networked ecosystem capable of addressing the full range of community needs without relying on predatory capitalism or government administrations more responsive to the interests of their largest donors than those of their most oppressed, disinherited constituents. Building an ecosystem at the regional level is a compelling scale and level of organizing. It is, of course, not the only scale at which organizing needs to take place; it is an especially appropriate level, given its strategic, middle ground between local and national scales of organizing.

Working at the regional level across multiple states, rather than concentrating within single states or at the neighborhood level, fills a gap that is sorely needed. Tons of organizations currently exist to organize for sustainable, systems-transitioning justice at the local level. But what is needed, among other things, are groups like the New Economy Coalition. Their advocacy and call for a regional flowering of solidarity economies is a viable path forward, one that aspires to create a democratic, community-guided economy in place of the bullying, coercive economy that we currently have.

Solidarity economies, at their best, provide a people-centered, values-driven model of organizing political and economic life that is both compatible with, and reflective of, faith traditions like Christianity.

PROTEST

Participatory democracy can include, at times, participation against government. This *against*-the-system work is the vein of disruptive protest, and it is often underappreciated.

What comes to mind here are Black folks demonstrating against broken levees during Hurricane Katrina and the summer protests of 2020 against the police-involved murders of George Floyd, Breonna Taylor, and Tony McDade, among others. Less publicized but no less important are the actions of citizens exercising their constitutional right to petition their government for the redress of grievances. Another example is students encouraging, and where needed, pressuring their schools to institute inclusive, academically engaging curricula that connects with and builds on their lived experiences.

Sometimes, participatory democracy looks like moral, nonviolent resistance to formal institutions of government in order to advance the common good

THE POWER OF LOVE

My own entrance into participatory democracy started as a Princeton Seminary student. Seminary was like a dream world for me: while enrolled, I felt baptized into a long-desired destination of formation, higher learning, and what felt like a rarefied world of contemplating church history, Scripture, Christian ethics, public theology, and more. After an exciting immersion into graduate theological education, I was hungry to go deeper. That opportunity came when I attended a three-night lecture series on the unfinished journey of America's spirit, delivered by then Newark mayor Cory Booker.

It was a heady time, during the first year of the Obama administration, when the wielding of presidential power by an African-American politician felt fresh, exciting, and almost vicarious. Many of us felt as though we were all in the White House with Barack, Michelle, Malia, Sasha, and Bo. In that context, Booker delivered a series of talks on the power of love as a motivating, sustaining force for public service to an enraptured audience. He painted a grassroots picture of civic organizations engaging in community problem solving, confronting mass incarceration, and supporting the reentry of formerly incarcerated folks back into society. He rhapsodized about the power of pluralism and the potential of "humble hopes and insane idealism" to address voting rights, secure genuine public safety, and providing family-sustaining, community uplifting structures of employment.

I experienced that series of lectures as a civic altar call. It prompted me to dive in to figure out how to participate in a plenty good room movement to make democracy work for everyone. That moment led me to benevolently badger the Mayor's Office in Newark until I secured a first-of-its-kind internship placement for a seminary student in their office, working on issues of public safety, green jobs, and the beautification of parks. That experience taught me that local governments can get a lot done. Local governments can restore parks, launch commissions to ensure LGBTQ communities' deeper inclusion in the political process, retain and attract grocery stores to food deserts, and the like.

I also learned that local governments are constrained by modest budgets and the state of macroeconomic environments. I learned how rare it is for political and community leaders to push for distributive justice and expanded access to public goods like education, housing, healthcare, fair employment, and decision-making power. Upon local communities, their governments, *and* their traditions of governance, much of the promise of democracy rises or falls.

Participation democracy fosters resilience and community confidence against long odds. I'm thinking here of Bishop William Barber's insistence that "every crucifixion needs a witness."[12] During a conversation with him at Yale in 2019, I was moved by his words: there may be times when we fail to win, but there must never be a time when we fail to bear witness. Social movement scholar Zeynep Tufekci makes a similar point when she notes that involvement in movements impacts not only the outcomes sought but the inward change felt by acting in concert with other human beings to change the systems that dominate and harm us. In the process, we strip those systems of their legitimacy.[13] In the wake of discredited systems and withdrawn belief in their effectiveness, we regain a golden opportunity: a chance to wager on the efficacy of divine-human partnership in rebuilding systems that actually serve us from the ruins of networks and institutions that have failed us.

What if all of us—not only politicians—are "elected" for public service? Suppose, for a moment, that entire communities possess the capacity to lead and create, to implement budgets, and to exercise the executive authority of making public choices, solving problems, and narrating the need for deep, continual social change. This design ideal informs innovations like participatory budgeting and community boards, both of which designate the power of public choice to ordinary residents and citizens. Such activities help accustom everyday folk to the bracing, beautiful work of collective self-governance.

To repair our democracy, we must reject the fiction that a small cadre of public servants deserve to wield the law and social power all by themselves. We must unmask and refute the myth of social salvation by individual effort. Governance is too precious, too sacred an activity to leave to civic officials alone. Community members in neighborhoods, congregation members in pews, and union members in group halls also have a critical role to play.

Participatory democracy is the preventive, upstream culture of engagement and involvement that aims to prevent problems before they take shape and need to be solved. When asked what advice he might give to clergy and people of conscience seeking to do justice, Rev. Adam Clayton Powell Jr., the former pastor of Abyssinian Baptist Church in Harlem and Harlem's legendary congressman, responded memorably and simply: involve yourselves.[14]

REPARATIVE DEMOCRACY

Alongside participatory democracy, reparative democracy presents another pathway for both correcting the shortcomings of representative democracy and harnessing its strengths.

Reparative democracy means that circles of changemakers, in small and large groups, identify, quantify, and redress historical wrongs in a spirit of covenant. Reparations and the practice of redressing identifiable, historic wrongs is a basic, fundamental part of self-government, despite the misrepresentations of its critics. Reparative democracy, as a foundational dimension of self-government, gives us an opportunity to unlearn America's rituals and routines of white supremacy. Unlearning white supremacy is about curating a political culture of radical candor and interdependence that seeks to understand how deep the wounds of anti-Black enslavement and its afterlife run. Redressing those wounds is essential to our democracy's survival and future.

Sustainable, comprehensive programs of reparations for Indigenous and African American communities are a leading example of reparative democracy. It is impossible to envision a morally credible, theologically defensible experiment in collective governance so long as stolen land, stolen labor, and therefore stolen opportunities have been stripped from Black and First Nation communities without substantive repair. This moral claim may not yet be common sense in our society, but reference points for the claim are all around us. As an example, the principle of legal recognition and repair for damages is well-established, despite not always being well-applied, in our court systems. Precedents for instituting reparations, as we considered previously, exist within our society. Given those two realities, reparations cannot be dismissed as unreasonable, since our legal system recognizes the core principle of the idea. Nor can reparations be dismissed as unworkable, since examples exist in local cities, academic institutions, and national contexts. The real objection to reparations, I suspect, is an anti-Black judgment about worth and unworthiness: Black and Indigenous people, according to the gaze of white supremacy, are not deemed valuable enough to fully redress the cross-generational wrongs committed in enslavement, land grabbing, and similar practices of social and moral evil.

Briefly reviewing the history and some of the objections to reparations helps to set the work of reparative democracy in context. Reparations now—as everyone from the Republic of New Afrika, to the Malcolm X Grassroots movement, to the Institute for Moral Political Economy, to Sandy Darity and similar stratification economists have argued—is a moral and civic demand that is a cornerstone of reparative democracy. Reparations now. Full stop.

But we can also make a bigger, bolder case. Reparative democracy is a constitutionally guaranteed practice encoded in the first amendment of the US Constitution, which recognizes in all of its citizens the right to petition the government for the redress of grievances. Boiled down to the basics, the redress of grievances translates into reparative activity.

Reparations, then, are not an exceptional mode of democratic activity, which we engage in only to solve egregious issues like enslavement, wrongful imprisonment, or faulty medicine that harms rather than heals. Reparative democracy sees reparative work not just as a once-and-done gesture of cash payment or government apology. Reparative activity, rather, is the expectation and ongoing practice of persons—and systems—committed to correcting wrongdoing, redistributing poorly allocated resources, and amending ill-designed laws and administrative codes. Reparative activity, moreover, is a sacred task. This work can take the form of using symbols, stories, and rituals—like the biblical story of Zacchaeus materially redressing individuals that he harmed—in order to name and repair the wounds that scar individuals, societies, and entire ecosystems.

What does everyday reparative activity look like? It's congregations and community organizers working to expunge individual records of justice-system-involved persons and redistribute opportunities for community-oriented enterprise to individuals who suffered incarceration. Reparative activities are city planning and zoning commissions redrawing land use maps to incorporate beautiful public parks—rather than threadbare traffic triangles and poorly kept patches of grass—to adorn the built environments of every neighborhood, beginning with institutionally underserved communities. Although it is sometimes rhetorically devalued, reparative activity is also the culturally enriching practice of honoring the lives and contributions of enslaved and emancipated persons. This might include building statues and historical markers and crafting public murals, including graffiti, to honor folks like Toni Morrison, Harriet Tubman, and Frederick Douglass as well as the communities and traditions that formed them.

Walter Brueggemann, the noted Hebrew Bible scholar, captures this insight when he noted that "justice is sorting out what belongs to whom and returning it to them."[15] The reparative rhythm of "sorting out what belongs to whom and returning it" is especially salient in the environmental justice movement. Investing in clean water and green, career-track jobs, for example, are complementary priorities that should be prioritized for communities hit hardest by industrial pollution, poor air quality, and untreated water; adopting this sort of priority helps to ensure that frontline communities benefit first as we transition our economy from fossil fuels to renewable energy. Similarly, we can cut greenhouse gas emissions and practice the mitigation and adaptive strategies of climate change with a reparative understanding of democracy. Coastal communities are hit first and hardest as a result of extreme weather patterns, and we can, if we so choose, prioritize mitigation in those areas with repair as a guiding ideal and metric of what effective, equitable work looks like.

Plenty good room moments of reparative democracy surround us. Historical reparations to Japanese Americans for internment camps offer one example. As we considered earlier, the imperfect yet noteworthy steps of Evanston to move toward reparations in housing are another. Princeton Seminary, my alma mater, has also taken beginning steps toward reparations by renaming select buildings, convening truth-and-reconciliation style research and commissions, and setting aside $28 million from its endowment to resource the work. These steps, while not yet giant strides, nevertheless illustrate both the magnitude of the challenge as well as the energizing power of swinging the axe against the root of racial injustice, to use the language of the biblical prophet John the Baptist. Such work, done deeply and consistently, better enables us to bear fruit in keeping with repentance.

In my twenties, I worked with a local environmental justice alliance, labor union groups, former elected officials, and congregations in New York City on reparative dimensions of environmental justice. In the Gotham of the time, commercial waste from offices, small businesses, and the like concentrated in communities of color—specifically the South Bronx, Southeast Queens, and North Brooklyn. Waste inequity is a life-threatening issue that places children and elders at greatest risk while posing direct harms to entire communities. To address these issues, we engage in sustained political and religious education. We organized a toxic tour of local waste sites, wrote op-eds and press releases, and combined salaried labor and volunteer labor to lead an effort to repair the environment for communities of color.

Our work ultimately resulted in the passage of a bill creating commercial waste zones in the city that better resolved the issue. Even as work remains to be done, each time we move the needle like this, we help to make the reparative strand of democracy a bit more real.

ECONOMIC DEMOCRACY

The final stream of democracy, economic democracy, builds on the streams of participatory and reparative democracy. Seen as a threefold strand, they correct the flaws of and build on the best of representative traditions of government. In an economic democracy, unions and other collectives of people steward the raw materials of our economy (land, technology, labor, and innovation) in a way that is adaptable and maximizes cooperation and equality. Enshrining democracy in government, while leaving top-down, investor-controlled governance in place in the private sector, holds the potential to create an apartheid society. Economic democracy, by contrast, strives to maximize collective decision-making and aims toward the North Star of a cooperative commonwealth rather than profit maximization and satisfying stockholder's desire for quarterly returns.

A few examples may help. The groundbreaking research of political economist Jessica Gordon Nembhard uncovers the reality that cooperatives are a longstanding tradition of economic decision-making within Black communities. Fannie Lou Hamer's work with the Freedom Farm Collaborative in Mississippi offers an example of what economic democracy looks like in real time. In 1969, Hamer founded the Freedom Farm Cooperative with a $10,000 donation.[16] As a result of her dedication, the Farm cooperative developed into what has been called "a multi-faceted self-help program" and purchased an additional 640 acres for cultivation. With funds from the National Council of Negro Women, the co-op helped to provide food security and self-sufficiency for impoverished families in Mississippi.[17] During an environment of intense civic repression, outright white supremacy, and widespread poverty in the Mississippi Delta, Hamer's cooperative established a measure of economic stability as long as it lasted. While the organization eventually closed its doors due to insufficient funding, its legacy of racial justice and group decision-making remains an inspiration to all who seek to build organizations that center human dignity and economic equity.

Cooperatives often struggle to secure sufficient capital, largely because public investment is minimal and because they pose a threat to the extractive, capitalist use of real estate, technology, information, and talent. As one strategy for addressing this ongoing challenge, pairing a cooperative expansion strategy with investment in public banks is a critical step to moving toward a more democratic, humane economy. It's also important to ensure that workforce development and small business service agencies in cities, towns, and state agencies prioritize greater democracy, worker voice, and incubation support for cooperative enterprise in our economy.

At the heart of economic democracy is the idea of co-creation: collaborative work on investment, planning, and management decisions, as well as problem solving, revenue generation, and leadership development. Instead of contingent employees, consultants, and entry-level staff executing what senior management dictates with as little variation as possible, economic democracy places co-creation in the hands of workers. Co-creation also means that credit unions, community development financial institutions (CDFIs), and public banks, rather than global, predatory institutions, serve as depository institutions for cities and towns.

We see plenty good room moments of economic democracy in the New Economy Coalition, as we considered earlier, and in the Transnational Institute, a think tank and advocacy institute committed to "building a just, democratic, and sustainable planet."[18] We see it in advocacy for public banks, community land trusts, and sovereign wealth funds with community mandates. These examples and models are not a grab bag of policy ideas and wish list items. They are, instead, components of a substantive vision to build a different, more equitable social order, one worthy of our allegiance, support, and humanity.

It is absurd to try to repair a faulty system unless it can actually be fixed—or rebuilt and fixed at the same time. I believe that every society and ecosystem in God's creation can be redesigned, reborn, and where the people so decide, undergo moral and cultural revolution, for the earth is still the Lord's and the fullest thereof; the people and they that dwell therein.[19]

WHEN JUSTICE ROLLS DOWN LIKE WATERS

Cooperation is a deeply biblical theme. It is present in Acts 2 and Acts 4, where the early church community is remembered as voluntarily pooling its possessions to meet the needs of their people. The writer of Acts narrates this activity with a definite value judgment: that is, the sign of the Spirit's presence among them is exhibited in their willingness to share their goods and assign them to the areas of greatest need.

There is a notable difference between voluntary cooperative activity and coerced cooperative activity. But the inescapable resemblance between the Acts portrait of community and Marx's dictum—"from each according to ability and to each according to their need"—is difficult to overlook.[20] Those who have plenty carry an obligation to share it with those who do not. There is no ancient justification for private property, or for enclosing public goods in the control of a tiny circle of elites. Neither is such a justification found in the book of Acts.

What we see in the Acts narrative instead is an imperfect yet inspiring—and attainable—model of living, working, and deciding together that no one should go without their needs met. The narrative illustrates the power, and the feasibility, of human interdependence and God's people moving toward realizing their full human rights. Those rights include the right to an abundant life, lived and shared in a thriving, collectively self-sufficient existence. With this spirit of repair in place, we can realize the three streams of democracy—participatory, reparative, and economic. In the process we can come closer to justice rolling down like water and righteousness like a mighty stream.

4 | FINDING BLACK CHRISTIAN SOCIALISM

Capitalism is increasingly derided in our moment. While some citizens and residents retain a positive view of capitalism, many people increasingly doubt the promise of a laissez-faire economy that purportedly harnesses the inequalities of the business cycle into a more productive, efficient use for society. Many dismiss our system's claims: that election cycles bring justice, that our economy is an equal playing field.

Yet few people openly articulate the dream of an alternate political economy—one that openly seeks to move beyond a harsh capitalism (or even its rebranded "do good and do well" edition). What will it take for us to move forward: from endless critiques of capitalism that impoverishes us all, to a better, more equitable, more sustainable vision of our common life? What blend of spirituality and political economy might open up a future in which all God's children experience plenty good room?

In 1980, Cornel West—who had not yet become a household name through the publication of *Race Matters*, which came fourteen years later—made a crucial contribution to this conversation by outlining the tradition of Black Christian socialism in *Witness* magazine, a flagship publication of the Episcopal church. Black Christian socialisms offer an inheritance of ideas, movements, and initiatives as resources for moving beyond the social miseries and distorted desires occasioned by the imperial work of racial capitalism. In this chapter we'll dive deeper into the history and potential of Black Christian socialism, rooting our discussion in a look at America's most famous democratic socialist, Rev. Dr. Martin Luther King Jr. First, however, let's look at the rise in socialism's popularity and its definitions.

AN IDEA WHOSE TIME HAS COME?

A 2011 study from the Pew Research Center indicates that socialism among millennials possesses more supporters than opponents. That year, 49 percent of millennials polled held a positive view of socialism; 43 percent, not so much. Notably, that same report indicated that 55 percent of Black folks held a positive view of socialism—a clear majority. A decade later, in 2022, another Pew study found slightly lower but still substantial support among young folks and Black folks. Roughly 44 percent of eighteen- to twenty-nine-year-olds in Generation Z view socialism positively; 52 percent of Black people—notably, still a majority—likewise view socialism in a positive light.[1]

Inferences from such studies—and others like it—have been overstated, but this much seems fair: the inequalities and externalities of capitalism have created a hearing for socialist arguments, campaigns, and strategies. The goal here is not to romanticize any and every version of democratic socialism. The historical records, across the centuries, across differing countries, is clear: no political system is entirely free from error, or capable of instituting comprehensive checks and balances on the overreach of state power and private economic wealth in determining how, where, and for whose benefit public resources and services are used. Still, each of us should consider picking a side. Each of us has the opportunity and obligation to make an informed, prayerful choice about which political economy best aligns with the substance and spirit of our faith traditions and ethical commitments.

Here's where I stand: a socialism that respects the investigative, educational power of the press, upholds the full range of civil liberties, and commits to a weaving of justice that unravels every strand of class exploitation, anti-Blackness, colonial design, gender oppression, and human hierarchy is the closest approximation of God's beloved community and peaceable society that humans can create and sustain.

WHAT IS SOCIALISM—AND WHAT IS IT *NOT*?

Defining socialism, at times, can feel like a meaningless debate about distinctions that don't make a difference. Reasoning together about what is meant by socialism, however, is important in order to counteract the deliberate misinformation, mislabeling, and outright fearmongering that discussions of socialism can generate. This process is surely in the spirit of the ancient Hebrew prophet Isaiah, who calls his hearers and original audience in Isaiah 1:18 to "come now, and let us reason together."

To arrive at workable, constructive, historically informed frameworks of socialism, we need to articulate what socialism does *not* mean. Such an exercise is crucial to undertake in order to promote, without prejudice or slogan-driven slander, what the project of a faith-rooted, culturally expansive, democratic socialism seeks to achieve.

I do not take socialism to necessarily mean the complete abolition of all forms of private property, contracts between individual parties, or the utter erasure of markets. Instead, socialism connotes meeting the needs of humans and our environment through public provision and protection, deep cooperative and public ownership, and private enterprise characterized by collective bargaining, co-determination, and government regulation. It also means that working individuals who produce goods and services have a significant say in shaping, owning, and influencing the institutions that shape their day-to-day quality of life.

Socialism, in many ways, is a socioeconomic system that channels the power of working families, that pushes for economic justice, and that trusts the critical thinking of the people to make up their own minds about political economy and their own role in it. But also, socialism in an American-style context, as Gary Dorrien has noted, emphasizes the importance of freedom, choice, and liberty not as a concession but in the fullest sense of what the term means. In an economically just society, families and community members can choose what sort of education or healthcare to pursue within the context of publicly guaranteed access to social goods. A good example of this would be the free vaccines made available to citizens during the pandemic. Individuals and families were free to schedule where and when they would obtain vaccines from among public goods that were completely underwritten by taxpayers.

What, then, is meant by socialism as I use it in this book? Socialism, on a basic level, prioritizes human rights over property rights and our obligations to one another over conventions about the natural, efficient operations of markets. Socialism means a way of making decisions about the generation and the use of resources that seeks to end preventable poverty, exploitation, and human misery more than turning an ever-increasing profit. It's an ethical vision that also entails shared sacrifice for mutual gain—for instance, paying more in taxes to support health care, education, and other services that are free at the point of access. Ultimately, repairing the foundations of our public life requires turning the page on a capitalism that occasionally consults its citizens on the decisions of its largest investors, donors, and industry leaders—we call these occasional consultations "elections"—and instead moving to a participatory socialism. Elections certainly have consequences, particularly in the case of ballot initiatives and legislative reforms. Yet without the redistribution of wealth, wider membership in unions, and the leveraging of public investment—the indispensable tools of fiscal policy and taxation, monetary policy, and trade policy—elections will remain a painfully piecemeal exercise in progress.

There's a personal dimension to all of this for me. When I was a young adult, I began to realize that another way of organizing land, labor, and capital is possible—and that it is already happening locally, regionally, and to some extent, nationally. Gar Alperovitz's book *What Must We Then Do?*, John Nichols's book *The "S" Word*, and Martin Luther King Jr.'s letters, interviews, and witness of a Black social gospel and democratic socialism all proved formative to me. After discovering such works, I began to see that community land trusts, a cooperative way of organizing land ownership, found their American origins in my home state of Georgia. That unique story of emergence led to the birth of efforts such as Habitat for Humanity, where I worked in my twenties; creative, place-specific interpretations of Scripture like the *Cotton Patch Gospel*; and other efforts to wager an interracial solidarity in the resolutely racist Jim Crow South.

A participatory socialism happens when everyday people help make choices—and unmake choices through the effective veto power of popular referenda—about our common life: from regional planning and social insurance to setting the agenda for local economic development. The recently conducted Strike for Black Lives, for example, mobilized more than sixty labor organizations across the country in coordinated worker walkouts from their jobs, illustrating the promise and social power of explicitly centering the wages and well-being of Black people in our polity.[2]

BLACK CHRISTIAN SOCIALISM

Cornel West argues that Black socialist theologians acknowledge that both white supremacy and class inequality create a "major obstacle which stands in the way of black enhancement."[3] By *black enhancement*, what is meant is improving the material and environmental conditions of black life, rather than an individualistic notion of upward mobility in status and financial position. With characteristic precision and distinction, West delineates a specific concept of class under socialism—namely, a "decentralized democratizing of the production process, not a vulgar leveling of incomes."[4]

West's point is a critical one, because it refutes some of the common misconceptions of how socialism views class inequality. Class analysis in a socialist method is not inherently based on envy, hatred, or resentment of those presumed to be more successful or wealthy. Class analysis and struggle, as West insightfully implies, is not about leading to the total leveling of differing tiers of status; it is about naming and confronting the fact that a wealthy few unjustly hold decision-making, narrative-controlling, and resource-allocating power over their poorer and lower-wealth siblings. Notwithstanding the strengths of West's analysis, it could be sharpened by dedicating more explicit attention to what Amaryah Armstrong terms the linkage between "law, order, and the economy" and the "black radical tradition." Armstrong persuasively argues two interrelated points: America's political economy is largely based on the "condemnation of blackness," and two, that arguments for economic justice that overlook the anti-black traditions of both capitalism and socialism can end up reinforcing white supremacy in the name of a supposedly universal liberation.[5] As a straightforward example of this, we might recall how debates of the 2016 presidential cycle positioned reparations for Black folks as a distraction from the work of democratic socialism. To be credible in our moment, Black Christian socialism must seek to understand "our material and spiritual history from the underside" and, from that place, endeavor to create a plenty good room society that transforms the environmental conditions and ways of interpreting the world which produce anti-blackness and capitalist exploitation.

Fair enough, you may be saying, but what precisely is Black Christian socialism? Black Christian socialism is many things, but it is at least this: an inclusive, reparative, economic democracy with enduring inspiration drawn from Jesus's words—"the Spirit of the Lord is upon me because he has anointed me to preach good news to the poor . . . release to the captives, recovery of sight to the blind, to let the oppressed go free."[6]

In 2017, I designed and taught an undergraduate seminar course at the City College of New York on economic justice and public policy in US cities. Among the topics covered, the syllabus included a two-week unit that covered the subject of socialism, less than a year after the 2016 election cycle. During that course, I offered a textbook definition of *socialism* containing two components. First, socialism is the public or social ownership of the means of production—think technology, real estate, information, capital—that guides the creation, allocation, and access, for communities, to critical goods and services. Second, socialism—at least in its democratic forms—seeks to undo racial injustice and all forms of minoritized oppression while emphasizing civil liberties such as the right to vote and the freedom of assembly as foundational to a vibrant, equitable society. Such freedoms are fundamental if working families in every community are to engage the public policy process with influence, equal civic authority, and decision-making power.

Grounding ourselves in the history of democratic socialism and Christian faith traditions is a worthwhile exercise. In the words of my former seminary professor of church history, Dr. Paul Rorem, "we study history because it gives us perspective; and perspective, once understood, gives us hope." To forge a cooperative commonwealth capable of transforming the current container of a capitalist, imperialist economy, we need an understanding of individuals and small groups working toward the abolition of classes, which is to say the abolition of white supremacy and structurally uneven power relations that result in domination and extraction of wealth, labor, identity, and time.

To set socialism in fuller context, it's helpful to look to America's most famous democratic socialist: Rev. Dr. Martin Luther King Jr.

AMERICA'S MOST FAMOUS DEMOCRATIC SOCIALIST

When Martin Luther King Jr. and Coretta Scott first began to date in Boston, their conversations were largely oriented around literature, politics, and the economy. In a 1952 note addressed to Coretta, Martin argued that "capitalism has outlived its usefulness" and that he has always been more socialistic in his economic theory than capitalistic.[7] In 1953, on a radio broadcast from Ebenezer Baptist Church in Atlanta, King offered a notable prayer, which is contained in a volume of King's prayers edited by Lewis Baldwin. "In the name and spirit of Jesus," King prayed that the church would "work with renewed vigor for a warless world, for a better distribution of wealth, and for a brotherhood that transcends race or color."[8]

This sampling of King's correspondence and prayers—in addition to the work of scholars like Andrew J. Douglas and Jared A. Loggins, who have researched King's material critique of racial capitalism—illustrates that King entered not only public ministry but also pastoral ministry with anti-capitalist commitments. In fact, an anti-capitalist thread holds together his quilted vision of the beloved community. King's commitments evolved over time, informed by his reading, movement work, travel, and inner circle. Nevertheless, King put his best anti-capitalist foot forward from the beginning.

Why is it worthwhile to name King's anti-capitalist commitments as a faith leader? Firstly, intellectual integrity demands that we take people on their own terms and in their own words. King's theological, rhetorical, and written correspondence suggests a deep suspicion of private property, inhumane housing, and an abiding concern for Black folks. King, like many Black Americans, was also concerned with what writer and activist Michael Harrington referred to in 1962 as "the other America."[9] King referred to these people as the ones living on a "lonely island of poverty in the midst of a vast ocean of material prosperity."[10]

Secondly, anyone who believes that the power of the gospel requires a confrontation with what the late New Testament scholar Walter Wink refers to as the "principalities and powers" look to King for inspiration. King, they maintain, showed us how to fight against the exploitation that is synonymous with capitalism.[11]

Additionally, by recognizing King's anti-capitalism, we are forced to undo what womanist ethicist Emilie M. Townes calls the "cultural production of evil," a process that misremembers King as an American exceptionalist who sought to redeem the soul of the nation by proposing a few tweaks and modifications rather than pushing for wholesale, systemic change.[12] In reality, this icon of US public life was a harsh critic of American exceptionalism and an even harsher critic of America's most sacred cow: the US economy.

As a staunch critic of the United States and its capitalist economy, King directly contradicts the decontextualized images that would flatten him and the civil rights movement into a single "I Have A Dream" speech. This decontextualization disfigures both King's theological commitments and the freedom faith of Rev. Dr. Prathia Hall who inspired the "dream" segment of the speech. King's full body of work—from his correspondence and prayers, to his sermons and writings—envisions a "person-oriented society" that values human rights over private property rights. His work deeply critiqued economic exploitation and preventable conditions of poverty in the wealthiest nation to ever exist.

Despite the evidence that clearly shows that King was a critic of both the United States and capitalism, we still see bad-faith portrayals of King. Politicians appeal to his legacy to support causes that he would not champion—such as criminalizing protest or generically praising him as an embodiment of America's founding ideals.

In addition to addressing misrepresentations of King, it's also important to charitably address inadvertent distortions of King's life, legacy, and letters. What I have in mind are invocations of King that sever his antiwar activism and commitment to voting rights from his commitment to a reconstructed economic order. King's vision of beloved community is not simply a churchy way to call for liberal democracy: fair voting, a free press, the right to assemble and protest, or a generous welfare state to supplant the fiscal austerity that emerged following his assassination. What King called for was a radical revolution of values that confronts the giant triplets of racism, materialism, and poverty that are built into the economic foundations of the United States's liberal democracy.

Princeton African American studies professor Keeanga Yamahtta-Taylor notes that King told the *New York Times* that he was engaged "in a kind of class struggle," which further confirms that King cannot be presented as a great American marching for a kinder, gentler free-market economy.[13] King, along with many others in the Black social gospel tradition that shaped him, embodied a socialist commitment that held together militant nonviolent protest against racial injustice and a deep vision of participatory democracy. This vision emerged from his theological and philosophical conviction that all of humanity is sacred.

These are the reasons I view King's faith and radical anti-capitalist politics as being inherently related. As a board member of the Institute for Christian Socialism and the former executive director of the Drum Major Institute, an organization co-founded by King and his lawyer, Harry H. Wachtel, I feel a personal commitment to ensuring that the practical implications of King's commitments are carried forward. Regardless of whether you have a personal connection to King's legacy, my hope is that we who take King's work seriously will hear him on his own terms, in his own words, and respond accordingly.

KING'S CHRISTIAN CALL

In *All Labor Has Dignity*, labor historian Michael Honey highlights some of the ways the practical implications of King's theopolitical commitments dovetail with anti-capitalist activism. Throughout his life, King argued a mixture of pragmatic points regarding a labor-religion-civil rights alliance. In a 1961 speech to the Detroit United Automobile Workers Union, King explained that "it is axiomatic that what labor needs, Negroes need, and simple logic therefore puts us side by side in the struggle for all elements in the decent standard of living."[14] Toward the end of King's life, he had become unmistakably vocal in labor organizing. In 1968, King traveled to Memphis to march with Black sanitation workers who were attempting to unionize in an effort to improve work conditions. The day after the march, April 4, 1968, King was assassinated.

To understand King's life and legacy, we must understand his activism in the context of his call as a minister. In 1956 a sermon titled "Paul's Letter to American Christians," King called for a "better distribution of wealth." He also asserted that "God never intended one people to live in superfluous inordinate wealth, while others live in abject deadening poverty."[15] Holistically interpreting King's theological work as a pastor, public theologian, and faith leader requires grounding his anti-capitalism in his self-identification as a minister of the Christian gospel.

Today, King's legacy as a pastor-theologian and activist-minister summons us to transition from a capitalist economy into a socialist economy. Such an economy values civil liberty, political freedoms, and a strongly circumscribed market with constraints imposed not only by law and public opinion but by social ownership, worker self-organization, and a coalition of people from varying faiths and conscientious positions who believe in the beloved community.

As we strive to build interracial, intercultural, and international alliances capable of turning the page on capitalism, colonialism, and patriarchy, King's legacy belongs to all of us. That's not to say King is above criticism. Indeed, as Shatema Threadcraft and Brandon Terry note, it is important to "think with King against King."[16] But it is equally important to remember that King's legacy does not belong to interpreters who seek to redact or selectively render his life and words for purposes that are incongruent with the life he actually led.

When we remember the living legacy of Rev. Dr. Martin Luther King Jr., direct service and personal moments of reflection have their place. But to truly value King's theological and ethical vision, let us organize, preach, vote, write, and agitate in a way that places anti-capitalism at the center of the beloved community. Let us place the construction of a fully decolonized world house at the center of our global neighborhood—one where unequal trade relations, enormous loan repayment burdens, and other material harms facing formerly colonized nations are abolished. The enormity of the odds may be steep, and the challenges before us formidable. Yet God still calls us, in the words of King, "to hew out of the mountain of despair, a stone of hope."[17]

WHiCH JESUS DO WE FOLLOW?

Dr. King's witness of Black Christian socialism leads us to consider the Christ at the center of "Christian." In our contentious moment, a variety of portraits about Jesus's ministry compete for the loyalty of those who steward his legacy. Such dueling depictions inevitably must face the question of how to assess the cross of Jesus. What effect does the cross have on the church, societies the world over, our families, all creation? We must also pay meticulous attention to what we mean when we say the name of Jesus. Who is Jesus to capitalists? To Christians who are democratic socialists? To all those who sympathize with efforts to build a plenty good room movement?

Embodying a many-sided theology of the cross is essential to building a genuinely inclusive plenty good room movement. For those of peace church traditions—the Quakers, the Mennonites and other Anabaptists, and the like—Jesus is crucified as a nonviolent priest who came preaching peace, whose priestly sacrifice reconciles humanity to God, and who puts an end to the centuries-old myth of redemptive violence. This tradition encourages us to revive the anti-imperial, anti-war witness of peace, founded on justice, as foundational to building a plenty good room movement.

There is also the important womanist critique of the cross, which asserts that talk about the cross too often glamorizes suffering and justifies the abuse of women, men, gender-expansive folks, and children. The womanist theological tradition of rejecting surrogacy (essentially, one person suffering for another) is both insightful on its own terms and particularly relevant to a Christian interpretation of democratic socialism on two fronts.

First, womanism supplies an internal basis of self-criticism and doing right by Black women to an American socialist tradition that has, too frequently, been wrong on what was once called "the race question"; wrong with respect to white women; and especially wrong with respect to Black women and other minoritized women. A hard *no* to every sort of class reductionism is something that can and must be offered in Jesus's name and in the spirit of the womanist theological tradition.

Secondly, womanist theological traditions often pair the critique of surrogacy with a powerful, positive vision of who and what Jesus Christ is all about. Consider, for example, how Delores Williams calls us to advance "the ministerial vision" of Jesus, which she names as: "the ethical ministry of words" like the beatitudes and parables; a "healing ministry of touch and being touched" like restored health when the leper was touched; and "militant ministry of expelling evil forces."[18] Importantly, Williams argues that Jesus's ministerial vision is grounded, again and again, in "the power of faith, prayer, compassion and love."[19] This kind of vision is not a dismissal of the transcendent and supernatural. It is, instead, a delightfully determined way of focusing our attention on God's full, blood-and-bone immersion within humanity.

The eternally radiant, once-lynched, now-alive presence of Jesus invites all those who seek his union into his tradition of anointed social work. Accepting this invitation, in our racist, capitalist age of authoritarian governments and wickedly uneven access to life-saving medicine and technology, might change everything. This sort of understanding has animated my own pathway to a persistent, soul-calming preoccupation with Jesus as the guide, the goal, and—because I'm a Black Baptist preacher—the guardian of my own life.

Jesus is, as the theologian Karl Barth might put it, "the partisan of the poor."[20] He is crucified because he redraws the traditional lines of intimacy in the God-humanity relationship. Instead of restricting God's closeness and identification to a small circle of humanity, Jesus insists on drawing a wider circle, proclaiming that God's way of running things demands identification with people who are labeled the least in our society. The compassionate career of Jesus repeatedly sides with people who are made invisible by dogma, scapegoating, and oppression. This Jesus calls us to the mutually healing obligation to love our neighbors as we love ourselves.

This Jesus is the world's most famous labor union leader, as we will see in the next chapter—one who recruits human beings to pledge their relationships, intelligence, resources, emotions, and labor (in a word, their faith)—to a unique fellowship. In this Jesus fellowship, a divine spirit of growth, wisdom, power, and solidarity inspires its members to reverse ancient patterns of social evil. And how is this work of reversal to be done? We do it, in part, through the reflective, risk-taking practices of prayer, mutual aid, and loving the human beings we encounter as stead-fastly and skillfully as we can manage.

Jesus told his followers in Matthew 7:7, "Ask and it will be given to you; seek and you will find; knock and the door will be opened to you." What would happen if we heeded Jesus's three-point micro-sermon of asking, seeking, and knocking with daring interpretation? We might *ask*: why is capitalism seen by some as the natural ally of Christianity when it has historically incentiv-ized explaining away the stolen land of indigenous people, the stolen labor of oppressed people, and now, a heating planet, as market opportunities for turning a profit? We might *seek* methods to make love as effective within the scope of society as it is within our sanctuaries and within the grand universe of our hearts and minds. And we might *knock* open closed doors of economic decision-making and opportunity, demanding equitable invest-ment in abandoned neighborhoods, votes for employees on boards of directors, and more.

Let us ask, seek, and knock, collaborating with the Spirit to love ourselves into the peaceful, productive, abundant relation-ality that Jesus incarnated and calls us to continue.

5 | TAKING COMMUNION, JOINING A UNION

Rev. Addie Wyatt spent her life creating plenty good room moments. As an ordained minister and civil rights activist, she worked with Chicago labor unions and became the first Black woman to hold a senior position—international vice president—in a national labor union. Her multi-city union leadership, across multiple states, is an example of creating plenty good room for the labor-oriented dimensions of the gospel to shine forth.[1]

In particular, Rev. Wyatt made a lasting contribution to Chicago's labor and to the civil rights movements by securing critical sources of funding for the Montgomery Bus Boycott. Through her leadership in what was then called the United Packinghouse Workers of America (UPWA), Wyatt helped her district raise $8,000 of the $11,000 total that the entire union raised.[2] As a result of her activism, Wyatt and Martin Luther King Jr. developed, according to biographer Marcia Walker-McWilliams, "a close relationship as spiritual leaders, civil rights activists, and proponents of working-class struggles."[3] With the support of Rev. Wyatt's UPWA and other unions pledging their legal support, fundraising, and people power, the people of Montgomery were able to create a carpooling system and alternate economy that sustained 381 days of resistance that leveled the old regime of segregation. With her support, the Montgomery Improvement Association, the NAACP, local congregations and community leaders helped open a new chapter of both civil rights and labor movement history.

When asked by an interviewer how she got started in labor organizing, Rev. Wyatt told a story of discrimination she and other Black women experienced in a factory in Chicago. "One of our greatest themes was to make life better for women," she said, going on to share:

> When I was working at Armour and Company, [I found out] that men made 14 cents an hour more than women working on the same line. I've always been a person from a child up to raise questions, why. And I raised that question, "Why?" And they told me it was because women didn't deserve to earn as much as men, and that women did not work as hard as men and they did not have to do heavy work like mine. Any more of that turned me on. It really turned me on. Because I guess one of the reasons it turned me on was because so many women felt that way too, not just me.

> We had to educate ourselves. We had to stir them up and we had to talk to our women about why we were really discriminated against. It has nothing to do with who has to do the more difficult jobs. It was because we were female and it was profitable to discriminate against somebody, and the somebodies that were discriminated against were those who were of color and those who were female.[4]

Rev. Addie Wyatt developed a holistic critique of the systems that were blunting her and her coworkers' life chances, their freedom. She asked why, while working alongside others to figure out the answer to her own question. As both a pastor and labor organizer, she understood, at an experiential level, how being a poor, Black woman multiplied the likelihood of suffering at the hands of racial capitalism. She knew that when we seek economic, racial, and gender equity, we can make plenty good room for a multidimensional experience of justice.

Rev. Wyatt knew that the work of building plenty good room for all is, fundamentally, not just a matter of politics, not just a matter of activism. The work of building an inclusive democratic socialism is, in deeply formative and sometimes frustrating ways, the work of piety, prayer, and invocation.

Rev. Addie Wyatt served a God who became a day laborer, a carpenter. Every time we protest an economy that divests from social services, social capital, and social justice while investing deeply in union-busting and ballooning budgets for the military and the police, our lives become enfleshed memorials to that laboring God. That divine presence, through Jesus, walked in the countryside and along seashores literally asking people to walk off their jobs and forge a countervailing community for the sake of God's creation and its freedom. He invited them to follow him, trust God to work through their effort, and help set everything wrong right, again and again.

A BRAIDED THEOLOGY OF JUSTICE

It's customary in some churches and in many protests to hear spirited critiques of what people call "all the isms." Down with capitalism! Down with sexism! Down with racism! The details are rarely spelled out, yet the underlying message is clear: injustice is a many-sided hydra. Defeating one of the heads, however, does not necessarily defeat evil altogether.

When we invoke the term *social justice*, what are we after? Will we know social justice when we see it? Here's one response: a braided theology of justice enables us to weave together the strands we know alongside the ones with which we are least familiar. As an example: I'm a cisgender, heterosexual Black man who experiences a fair amount of educational privilege and occupational status. Weaving a braided theology of justice, in my case, might mean cultivating a deeper analysis of, alertness to, and corrective action on sexuality, ability, gender, and educational access into my work of justice. For a same-gender loving, adult Black woman, weaving a braided theology of justice might mean learning from and with children, gender-nonconforming folks, and elders about how they embody justice.

The ideal in view here is not "political correctness" but, rather, deep listening and respect for self-determination as an act of loving oneself. The ideal being invoked here is also not identity politics, in the sense that the term is commonly used today. Identity politics in everyday conversation refers to a zero-sum, scarcity-oriented belief that one group's gain is necessarily another group's loss. This idea of identity politics is both false and ahistorical, stripping the paradigm from its crucial, originating context in the Combahee River Collective.

In 1977, the Collective pioneered the use of identity politics and an interlocking (rather than zero-sum) theory of oppression, famously arguing, "As Black women we see Black feminism as the logical political movement to combat the manifold and simultaneous oppressions that all women of color face."[5] To ensure clarity about their politics, they noted, "The most general statement of our politics at the present time would be that we are actively committed to struggling against racial, sexual, hetero-sexual, and class oppression, and see as our particular task the development of integrated analysis and practice based upon the fact that the major systems of oppression are interlocking."[6] The Collective's focus on interlocking oppressions, and on identity as a *catalyst* for rather than an *impediment* to organizing, contains lessons for us. We must weave together a braided theology of justice that can build and sustain a plenty good room movement. And that movement must be deeply pluralist and committed to belonging for all, so that participants can affirm all of who they are, while working for a world beyond racial capitalism.

THE FIRST LABOR UNION

Think about the early Christian movement for a bit. Jesus is a carpenter. Many of the disciples are marginally or lightly employed, focusing almost their entire talent, ability, and rela-tional interest into a permanently invitational fellowship that becomes the church. Jesus gathers them into a group of health-care workers, preachers, prayer warriors, and community organizers who pool material resources—like two fish and five loaves, cloaks, and tunics—and other essentials they might need. Together, they co-create a society committed to a Creator and a Christ calling them to hunger for justice, make peace, heal the sick, preach good news to the poor. They do all of this in a time in which literacy is virtually nonexistent and in which hearing and speaking are the major modes of communication. They do all of this in a world prior to the wage-labor system, on the edges of the client-patronage system of farming. Additionally, the early Jesus movement strikes a pragmatic stance: paying tribute to a political authority while retaining enough for one's family, tribe, and friends through cultivating a common purse.

Once the high-impact, high-trust fellowship of Christ forms, they pledge to one another their love, the complete measure of their labor, even their very lives. Such was the commitment and coalition of the early Jesus movement at its best.

What if we, too, are part of this divine-human labor union? Such a union is unbreakable by corporate intimidation. It cannot be co-opted by political parties. Those of us who are a part of this union are unabashedly committed to being partisans of the poor, the disinherited, and all those made insecure by the impersonal, amoral cruelties of business cycles and electoral cycles alike.

The sacred image of the communion table symbolizes the work of this labor union. I value greatly the meaning of the table as a call to remembering the work of Jesus in our prayer, in the ministry of local churches, and in their denominational and ecumenical expressions. The work of the communion, that holy meal, is the embodied celebration of God's labor union. Every time we eat and sit down at a table, we do it in remembrance of the Christ of day laborers.

When we fail workers at the bargaining table, we betray the moral imagination of the Christ who promises rest to the weary and heavy laden. Christ, after all, was a carpenter assembling a roving labor union of movement chaplains. Those chaplains—we often call them disciples—were part social workers, part prayer workers, part healers, part medicine men and women.

Some may object to this idea of the church as a labor union. They may point out that class differentiation in the church is simply too great to permit such a designation. Not everyone in the church is poor, and many are far from it. My response is that labor unions and worker centers alike have divisions of labor and some measure of hierarchy—hopefully minimal but nonetheless present. A church can have members in differing occupational levels and positions yet still remain true to its labor union roots.

What's required for the church to be a labor union is to provide structural support and advocacy for the working lives of its people. And for those who believe in the Christian story and its embodiment, where else but in church can we find job fairs and prayerful support to help those seeking employment? Where else can we find both college scholarships and the elders who celebrate young people as if they were their own children? Where else can we go for support in vocational discernment and identifying one's passion and purpose? Many churches today remain true to the call of Jesus to hunger after justice and preach good news to the poor.

An increasing number of denominations, congregations, and interfaith networks—such as Faith in Action, Direct Action Research Training Center (DART), Industrial Areas Foundation (IAF), and Gamaliel—are mobilizing a national and regional infrastructure on behalf of worker justice, voter activation, political self-determination, and higher wages. They are applying public pressure to make employment safer and more accessible to citizens and residents in our local communities. This reality is burgeoning, and it's hopeful. Local congregations could offer tremendous support by working in partnership with local worker centers, labor unions, and community development financial institutions.

Here's the take-home point: wherever we practice the art of association and assembly with coworkers, in a mood influenced by the spirit of the always compassionate and sometimes contrarian Christ, there we are carrying forward the labor union of our Lord.

COMMUNION

I've always been fascinated by the Lord's Supper. As a Baptist pastor committed to the communion table as a ritual of self-examination and meditation on the legacy and labor of the Christ, I find the sacrament extremely moving.

I understand, however, that the table may not hold the same meaning for other folks. Here's a way that folks who do not observe communion might be able to appreciate the radical meaning and potential of the ritual: communion is a time of vindication for a once-enslaved, once-lynched, now-exalted prayer warrior and high priest of restorative justice. Communion—that holy meal at the table that Jesus, in the last days before the crucifixion and resurrection, called us to share—is the embodied celebration of God's labor union. Communion is threatening enough to the powers that be that Oscar Romero, a Salvadoran priest who has become a kind of patron saint of liberation theology, was assassinated while administering communion in the spirit of the radical sense we are talking about here.

Fannie Lou Hamer used to call the communion table (referring to the civil rights movement) "God's welcoming table," a point drawn out by historian Charles Marsh.[7] That insight has stuck with me. What is communion if not God continually welcoming the shut out, overlooked, and excluded to the table?

For Christians, Jesus's teachings—on peacemaking and justice-hunger, on wagering one's life on God's provision and on close-knit religious fellowship—continue to jump off the pages of Bibles. But his words can captivate the spirit of anyone, seizing their imaginations and turning them toward a wide-open future.

For those who believe, Jesus is a high priest and a social worker, both Emmanuel and Son of God. He is labor union agitator, leader of the enslaved, a debt-canceling Savior. This unlikely one—this overlooked human being, this man of sorrows, this friend of the unhoused who himself was unhoused—is an ever-present Christ. He resides within the heart of every revolutionary who loves their enemies, their neighbors, and themselves at once.

Our beliefs about Jesus always reveal as much about us as they do about the Christ we follow. In that spirit, let's press the labor union line of reasoning a bit further. The gig-working Christ—who goes from town to town providing gospel hope and embodied healing—can supply inspiration to union drives, to living wage campaigns, and to all efforts that seek further authority and decision-making power for the disinherited.

If the twelve disciples can sit at the table with Jesus—one who would betray him, one who would deny him, the others who would desert him—from which negotiating, bargaining, or coalition table can any child of God be excluded? None.

To the extent that anyone is barred from a seat at a table, we need to consider whether the table-flipping Christ might suggest that table be flipped. There is plenty good room for all at the Eucharistic table. And there ought to be plenty good room for all at any table where decisions about resource generation, allocation, and investment are being made.

Which tables in your community disallow certain people from sitting at them? Which are thus candidates for being flipped over? At which tables might you take a seat?

Walking in the footsteps of our gig-working Savior, we can find common cause with anyone who seeks plenty good room for all. Along with Rev. Addie Wyatt, we can both join the union and take communion, finding within those places a hidden source of our strength and joy.

6 | BUILDING A PEOPLE'S ECONOMY

What if I told you that experiments in creating plenty good room exist all around us?

Throughout history, a wide range of experiments in crafting a people's economy have existed. Some of those examples are right under our nose, and we've looked at several in previous chapters. A cooperative economy in Montgomery, Alabama, which existed for nearly 381 days, helped make the Montgomery Bus Boycott possible. Underneath the withdrawal of participation from public busing, Black residents created a complex system of carpooling rides, cooking meals, administering a grassroots system of marketing through churches and community centers and more. In a 1907 Atlanta conference on economic cooperation among African Americans, sociologist W. E. B. Du Bois outlined the emergence of a people's economy in nascent form.[1] Within that outline, he included: banks and cooperative benevolence organizations, insurance societies, the social enterprises of churches, and what he called the "group economy." While the social world that Du Bois describes emerged in the setting of Jim Crow segregation, the patterns and practice of group economics from the early twentieth century contain lessons for the cultivation of a people's economy today.

One of the foremost scholars of a people's economy, Jessica Gordon Nembhard, spells out some of these practices and patterns in *Collective Courage: An African-American Cooperative Economic History*. Nembhard's book offers the definitive timeline of Black endeavors to forge a people's economy, spanning from 1780 to 2012 and encompassing industries as varied as bicycle repair shops and grocery stores to the Cooperative Home Care Associates, a South Bronx worker-owned cooperative founded in 1985, which is among the nation's largest worker cooperatives.

Du Bois's vision and Nembhard's research remind us that contemporary efforts to establish a people's economy build on a rich foundation. That foundation is not a static, dead past but a sacred, living tradition. It's a tradition of confronting both white supremacy and the politically engineered exclusion from resources through engaging in the economic and cultural work of planning, producing, and distributing the things that Black folks need for a fulfilling, thriving life. What is true of the best of Black folks' historical attempts to create people's economies is simultaneously a prism and precondition for creating a people's economy among any people. Attempts to build a people's economy in our decade and beyond must draw from the long, beautifully stubborn histories of Black folk creating socioeconomic models of provision and resource coordination. These models have sought—and still seek—to correct the ongoing, planetwide legacies of colonization, enslavement, broken treaties, and extraction of ancestral-community wealth for empires.

Let's zoom out a bit and ask the question: What does it look like to create a people's economy at a society-wide level? There are at least six pillars of a people's economy. Those pillars include: 1) pre-distribution, 2) redistribution, 3) co-determination, 4) social movement unionism, 5) communal ownership and stewardship of means of production, and 6) creative, meaningful work. We need to establish these key pillars of a people's economy in order to confront and replace the reign of racial capitalism. Economies should be organized to serve the needs and conditions of human beings and local ecosystems, not an ever-expanding geography of profits. Building a people's economy is not an unreachable ideal but a project rooted in sacred tradition and proud history. We turn now to these six pillars.

PILLAR 1: PRE-DISTRIBUTION

Creating and stewarding a *cooperative commonwealth*, as socialism is sometimes called, means being attentive and directive to both the *redistribution* of wealth from the top to those who co-create it at the bottom—that is, a multiracial, working-class, cross-generational population and electorate—and to the *pre-distribution* of income, benefits, and other forms of compensation flowing to working people.

Pre-distribution happens through resource allocation shifts *prior* to the tax and transfer system—for instance, by increasing the minimum wage to a living wage that enables compensation to help support a family, save for a rainy day, and create a measure of self-determination.[2] Another example of pre-distribution is compensation like paid sick leave, parental leave, sabbaticals, and other sorts of care policies encoded in law, promoted by the relevant agencies, and implemented at the organizational level.

The pre-distribution of income, paid leave, and capital investment happens through foundational factors like workplace organizing and shareholder activism, as well as crucial items like flexible, predictable scheduling, a living wage, and healthy, safe working conditions.

Focusing on the pre-distribution of income, workplace conditions, and retirement support, in tandem with a traditional focus on redistribution, can strengthen socialist work in its policy-making, legislating, and labor-organizing dimensions. The work of meeting human needs is far too important to be restricted to policy platforms during election cycles, the important-yet-hard-to-fully-predict trajectory of movement-building, or even the crucial work of asset-based community development by congregations and communities. The majority of families and individuals work in or are directly impacted by jobs that provide salaried, contracted, or informally transferred compensation. In terms of numerical reach, a pre-distribution lens focuses here, on our working lives, even as it supports electoral justice, movement-building, and community development as critical social functions.

With regard to workplace routines and rewards, racial capitalism imposes a rough, invisible logic: a dominant, rich cohort captures most of the rewards, while praising the "essential work" of those whose routines are most responsible for creating the rewards. A pre-distribution lens makes that harsh calculus plain to a mass audience so that it can be opposed and reformulated in a more equitable, transparent system.

This focus on pre-distribution is informed by ancient, biblical sources of inspiration. Among such sources are St. Paul's ethical insistence that the laborer deserves to be paid, and that all apostles, including himself, should meet the needs of the poor through their ministerial work.[3] Equally relevant is the contention, in the biblical epistle of James, that wage theft should be prevented.[4] Such first-century insights, and their underlying moral assessments, are upheld through twentieth-century instruments like labor protections, strong unions, and worker centers, and responsive departments of labor and workplace health.

PILLAR 2: REDISTRIBUTION

Redistribution refers to tax and transfer policies, usually carried out by legislatures and agencies, which assess a contribution from households and organizations in order to reallocate that assessment to another part of society. Income taxes are perhaps the most well-known example of redistribution, functioning on a graduated basis whereby the rich pay more than the poorest community members, in an escalating scale of brackets. The moral and operational justification for this arrangement is that the more affluent have generally gained more from society and are therefore best suited to contribute the highest amounts.

Redistribution contains both public and private examples. In a public sense, redistribution refers to programs of social insurance like unemployment insurance, social security, workers' compensation, and disability insurance. The idea of redistribution is that society expresses its compassion and sense of justice—my preferred term is what Ruth Wilson Gilmore calls a "social wage"—by dedicating resources to the welfare of its members, especially during vulnerable periods like old age, sickness, disability, and unemployment.[5] Redistribution advances a people's economy by taxing household and corporate wealth in order to allocate opportunity, critical public services, and programming to the most vulnerable and to the entirety of society.

Redistribution also contains a private dimension as well. Edgar Villaneuva, activist and author of *Decolonizing Wealth*, alludes to that function when he talks about how the philanthropic sector, individual donors and wealthy families and foundations, can decolonize wealth. Redistribution by philanthropy could be seen as pre-distribution, since it doesn't pass through the tax and transfer system of fiscal policy that governments run. However, categorizing philanthropic investment as redistribution makes more sense when we note that some institutional foundations, family trusts, and donor collectives hold more wealth than the GDP of entire nation-states. This dimension of redistribution asserts that all philanthropic communities have a moral duty to pool their resources and allocate them toward abolishing the socioeconomic conditions and political imbalances of power that create the need for charity in the first place. The work of organizations like Regeneration, the Solidaire Network, and Villanueva's Decolonizing Wealth Project, to name a few, exemplify the voluntary, collective redistribution of wealth and decision-making power. They move away from traditional philanthropy into the work of repairing democracy, building social movements, and ultimately, aiding the curation of a society of plenty good room for everyone.

Social insurance provides another frequently cited example of redistribution policy. While the most traditional programs refer to Medicare, Social Security, unemployment insurance, workers' compensation, and disability insurance, a wider program encompasses categories like education and workforce development; health; income support; and nutrition and shelter.[6] The purpose of such programs is to tax earnings in order to provide a stronger measure of economic security to individuals and families, particularly when illness, death, difficulties of aging, and similar incidents occur.

PILLAR 3: CO-DETERMINATION

Co-determination represents the third pillar of a people's economy. In theological and ethical terms, this idea means that persons formed in God's image—that is, everyone—deserves to have enough information and voice to meaningfully participate in the decisions and governance of their organizations. Typically, this vision is realized by establishing or increasing worker representation on a board of directors.[7] The principle of co-determination is also approximated by organizational models like workers' councils, worker cooperatives, mutual aid collectives, and unmet needs roundtables, which prioritize making choices about resource allocation based on consensus rather than deference and hierarchy.

Examples of co-determination are within reach. In the 1980s and 1990s, the US Steel Workers Union negotiated board representation for its workers; Pan American Airlines also agreed to worker representation on its board during this same time period.[8] Additionally, federal bills such as the Reward Work Act, while not enacted, have sought to introduce and further enshrine co-determination into US labor laws. Law professors Matthew Bodie and Grant Hayden make a blunt, affirmative case for co-determination, portraying the principle as a counterweight to the "principle of shareholder primacy." Shareholders, they claim, dominate decision-making in the United States to such an extent that they are effectively "the sole voting group within the corporate republic."[9]

Bodin and Hayden press the point further, arguing that "without worker participation in governance, companies can and do lobby for anti-worker legislation, discourage workers from joining unions, permanently replace striking workers in the interests of their shareholder polity, and view workers as simply an input into the production function."[10] Co-determination counteracts this kind of shareholder primacy by insisting that workers, the environment, and all stakeholders—not simply investors—deserve to be centered in governance culture and decision-making. Co-determination is an essential pillar of a people's economy because it ensures that the people themselves—not simply a group of professionals or subject-matter experts talking *about* the people—are co-creating their economic future.

PILLAR 4: SOCIAL MOVEMENT UNIONISM

Social movement unions advocate not only for the benefit of their members, as traditional labor unions might; they also advocate for the liberation of all members of a given community and society at large. Rather than bargaining predominantly for the advantage of their members relative to investors and managers, social movement unions at their best can initiate and sustain strikes, negotiate hard for fair contracts and worker benefits, intervene in elections for racially and economically just outcomes, and organize for a more equitable democracy, without which no victory at the workplace can be preserved over time.

Here's one example of economically just outcomes. The Service Employees International Union (SEIU) spent nearly a decade educating and agitating for living wages and union representation, spurred on first by courageous employees, most of them people of color, at a New York McDonald's. They won a historic victory. In a similar vein, Starbucks Workers United, the Amazon Labor Union, and flight attendant unions have each exercised a simultaneous commitment to protecting the financial futures and livelihoods of their members, as well as furthering the advancement of movements like the Poor People's Campaign: A National Call for Moral Revival, led by Rev. Dr. Liz Theoharis and Bishop William J. Barber II. We also see social movement unions cultivating a larger movement ecosystem through convening conferences like Labor Notes and outlets like *In These Times*, a labor-focused magazine expressly committed to democratic socialism and creating more humane, ecologically responsible societies.

Movement-oriented unions can help create a people's economy by preserving the concurrently productive and disruptive dimension of workplace organizing. As the one-time president of the board of directors for a statewide labor-religion coalition in New York, I have witnessed and contributed to this kind of workplace organizing. While they're not perfect, unions that are in touch with their radical roots can build commitment to rearrange an economy whose distorted wage scales, lopsided taxation, and misshapen monetary policy have taken a hammer to working families across distinctions of race, class, gender identity, age, and geography. The early efforts of the Congress of Industrial Organizing in the 1930s represented this tradition in the early twentieth century; in some ways, groups like the Chicago Teacher's Union, Domestic Workers United, National Nurses United, and numerous others represent this tradition in the twenty-first century. At their best, unions seek to craft a just future for an entire population, based on a moral commitment to their members, their sectors, and society as a whole.

Since the advent of neoliberalism in the 1970s, with its doctrinaire stance of privatization, slashing public services, and blunting the strength of labor unions, participation in the labor movement has fallen to an all-time low in the United States.[11] As of 2022, 10.1 percent of all US workers reported being in a union, compared with 20.1 percent of workers in 1983. That stark difference, unfortunately, both indicates the need to organize and demonstrates the structural weakness of the labor movement in America. These realities notwithstanding, the impact of unions is frequently overlooked and understated in popular understandings of what it takes to create a just society.

Our times require active, cross-sector organizing, with both vision and urgency. Social movement unionism means being committed to justice and to lesser-known yet deeply impactful campaigns and organizations like Wages for Housework and Domestic Workers United. Realizing an economy that is truly nonviolent and genuinely democratic requires rebuilding labor unions that protect the full spectrum of work: the salaried work of professionals, the labors of hourly workers, the gig work of freelancers, the unwaged work of the care economy, and dimensions yet to be named.

PILLAR 5: COMMUNAL OWNERSHIP AND STEWARDSHIP

Community and public ownership of productive land, technology, and social assets is a stabilizing anchor within a people's economy. Food provides an excellent example. Think about the quality of fresh food that can emerge from community-supported agriculture, local gardens, food co-ops, and farmers' markets. At a regional level, we could point to social assets like airports, seaports, navy yards, and industrial real estate as space whose use should be determined by voters, community members, and neighbors—not the consumer-driven identity promoted by the insistent marketing and commercials of racial capitalism. Community ownership is available in large and small examples, ranging from the Green Bay Packers' status as a publicly owned structure to the public ownership of hospitals and convention centers.

Community ownership is a protective strategy against a risky and historically documented practice of corporations: the closing down of their operations in search of lower production costs, less regulation, higher profits. Multinational corporations, with their limited attachments to local communities, lose little to nothing when they pick up and leave a community. When communities own their social assets—such as hospitals, community health centers, and local pharmacies—things like healthcare apartheid can be interrupted and systems that build toward public health can be created and sustained.

Community and public ownership, moreover, help make a people's economy possible by ensuring that people are not alienated from their local surroundings and from a sense of place in the world. As we considered in chapter 1, a sense of home—of belonging and rootedness—is a crucial dimension of communities that extend plenty good room. This kind of belonging helps us to build toward environments of deep, responsible stewardship. Social ownership ties production of goods and services to demands that actually exist in communities and households.

For example, Equal Exchange—a for-profit, fair trade, worker-owned cooperative—has created a more even playing field for growers of coffee and chocolate. In a similar way, neighborhoods and workers can create a more even, worker-led playing field across industries and in fields like technology through use of apps, online distribution channels, and so on.

PILLAR 6: CREATIVE, MEANINGFUL WORK

Creative work plays a hidden yet essential role in the co-creation of a people's economy. This dimension of a people's economy is about ensuring that work itself retains a measure of fulfillment, passion, and inventiveness. Rev. Dr. Katie Geneva Cannon, one of the founding voices of womanist theology and ethics, spoke about this when she described work and calling as "doing the work our souls must have."[12] In a similar vein, Rev. Dr. Martin Luther King Jr. spoke to this dimension of work when he remarked that "all labor has dignity."[13] From sanitation to software engineering, every occupation possesses a demanding, rewarding aspect that requires intelligence, creativity, and technique. With the business press focusing readers' attention on stock market performance, luxury taste, and the latest industry trends, the value of work as a spiritual, embodied undertaking often falls out of the picture.

Articulating the spiritual underpinnings of work is risky. It's susceptible to weaponized narratives that counsel overworked, underpaid laborers to "find their purpose" in patently unjust conditions. Such talk of spirituality deserves condemnation, satire, and dismissal. On the other hand, the spirituals, blues, and work songs created on the plantations and farmland of the Deep South illustrate that meaning and value and art can be created in brutalizing labor conditions without romanticizing the setting in which the art is formed.

The theological idea of the Spirit distributing gifts and abilities to all humans provides another foundation for conveying this idea. If human talent is God-given, then a primary aim of work is to mirror divine goodness by passionately, collaboratively, and skillfully doing what is useful to humanity, the environment, and its ecosystems.

Building a people's economy, with the six foregoing pillars in mind, is a proposition that will take active redesign, commitment to identifying the beauty within struggle, and fidelity to fulfilling the promise of reparative, economic democracy. It is also a prayer whose *amen* is found not only in the words of our mouth but in the work of our hands in community. The promise of reparative democracy also gives us an opportunity to unlearn America's rituals and routines of white supremacy. Undoing white supremacy, in turn, is about curating a political culture of radical candor and interdependence that seeks to understand how deep the wounds of anti-Black enslavement and its afterlife run. Redressing those wounds is essential to our democracy—and to our economy's future.

Now that we have looked at the six pillars of a people's economy, we turn, finally, toward strategies for co-creating plenty good room for all. The idea of plenty good room for all is one that turns the prevailing wisdom of racial capitalism upside down. Turning the world upside down is an urgent call of faith, one that summons commitment from the deepest chambers of our intuition, instinct, and imagination. It's a call that emerges from our conscience; that inspires us through careful, consistent study of history and its precedents; and that beckons us forward as we examine and engage in the world we inhabit.

7 | TURNING THE WORLD UPSIDE DOWN

Now is the moment for churches, our culture, and our communities to part ways with racial capitalism and its cousins: imperialism, male dominance, and hierarchy-obsessed religion. To part ways with such ingrained social patterns, and the desires they ignite, we need a multiracial, multigenerational, working-class movement that votes, organizes, prays, and when necessary, strikes. Together, we can begin to turn the world upside down.

While this vision of social reversal is as current as a push alert on a cell phone, it is ancient as well. An inspiring, mobilizing vision of salvation—of the world healed and fully enjoying the Spirit in a democratic and spiritual, rather than solely dogmatic, sense—led the disciples and early church community depicted in Acts to "turn the world upside down."[1]

"Philosophers have nurtured the world in various ways," Karl Marx once famously noted. "The point, however, is to change it."[2] The purpose of understanding racial injustice, class oppression, and cultural othering is so that we can turn the world upside down. And as we turn the world as we know it upside down, we actually make it right side up for everyone, beginning with the most vulnerable, with those most harmed by disenfranchisement, economic dispossession, interpersonal microaggressions, and other social evils.

In our moment, our call is similar to what both Marx and the book of Acts described: we study the wrongdoings of the world so that we can better understand how to do *right* by each other, in interpersonal, structural, and environmental ways. This is not a generalized call to do right. The myriad legacies of wrongdoing that fly under the banner of a beautiful ideal require more detail. Grammy and Oscar award–winning rapper Common addressed this reality through lyrics that poignantly argue: "justice for all just ain't specific enough."[3]

So in this chapter, we get specific. We know that building a plenty good room movement means building economic democracy in a way that overturns the legacies of anti-Blackness and the long shadow of the plantation. We know that co-creating a non-extractive society means abolishing the virtually omnipresent yet concealed patterns of patriarchy. Turning upside down the world of imperialism, capitalism, and heteropatriarchy—as the best of the Jesus movement and other traditions of faith have long sought to do—will involve specific steps.

Putting this world right side up is more than a matter of undoing old institutions and systems of injustice and endeavoring to build new ones. It's also about exposing and debunking false narratives in order to heal our society from what Dr. Emilie Townes calls "the cultural production of evil."[4] To that end, some of the ideas in this chapter, while they may be unfamiliar or seem unwieldy, will help us name the false narratives that surround us and commit ourselves to fuller, truer stories.

Why, exactly, do we need to turn the economy upside down? For one thing, the burdens and runaway prices of America's economy—which, at 26-plus trillion in gross domestic product (GDP) as of 2023, is the largest economy in the world—impose environmental hardship and injuries like disproportionately high rates of asthma, commercial waste, and polluting power plants in poor and low-wealth households across the country.[5] These adverse realities outstrip whatever technological breakthroughs and innovations may be experienced within capitalist societies.

We also need to turn the economy upside down because racialized capitalism gives us the false idea that supply-side economics will rain down economic mobility, financial empowerment, and greater self-determination for Black working-class folks. This idea may appear to be a caricature of an opposing view, but sometimes the truth is stranger than fiction: the Nobel-prize winning economist Milton Friedman once claimed: "There is one and only one social responsibility of business—to use its resources and engage in activities designed to increase its profits so long as it stays within the rules of the game, which is to say, engages in open and free competition without deception or fraud."[6] Versions of Friedman's idea still hold purchase in some quarters, undergirding pushback against even a patina of environmental responsibility or corporate engagement, let alone moving comprehensively toward an equitable economy. In contrast to such claims, we can set forth a counterargument: very low-income households cannot, en masse, experience better living conditions without strong legal protections for workers, deeper public investment in basic social goods, union organizing that brings back collective bargaining, and a system of more robust social insurance to which everyone contributes and from which everyone benefits.[7]

Until we say *no* to racialized capitalism and its corresponding hierarchies, the sounds of weekend worship will dull when the stock market bell tolls on Monday. We neglect the vision of a just, loving God when we think that simply making more middle-class folk of color will necessarily result in the liberation of first-generation college students and those who either choose not to or cannot access postsecondary education. There is more to be done beyond issuing a resolute *no* to an economy stratified by race and gender—one where Black women, despite being the most educated demographic among American workers, need to work sixty-six years to earn what white men make in forty years for comparable work.[8] For genuine, culturally relevant spiritual formation to happen, and for constructive experiments to transform our top-down economy, the *no* must come first.

Undoing the influences of racialized capitalism will take more than verbally affirming another world into being. It will take more than political education, as essential as that is. It will also require more than engaging policy advocacy and legislative lobbying, as essential as those tasks are. It will take turning over our conventional ideas about how the world is structured and setting in its place a new, more emancipatory common sense.

I am arguing against the tide of building just a more enlightened version of capitalism. I do not believe such theory of change is workable. Pretending that capitalism can be made more "humane" or "compassionate" prevents us from demanding impossible policies until the conditions of operationalizing the impossible becomes inevitable.

Can the impossible become the inevitable? Yes. Think of the hard-fought, zig-zag movement that led to nineteenth-century abolitionists ending slavery through the Civil War. Think, too, of the general strike by Black workers and their taking up of arms in the Union cause that led to an interlude of freedom.[9] Remember, too, the working-class movement to secure the franchise by Black folks in the March on Washington and the larger struggle for civil rights. Think of the plenty good room moments we've looked at in previous chapters. Each of those movements inched us from the impossible to the inevitable. Each of those individuals and network had to make, and sustain, what we could call a plenty good movement decision. My hope is that by reading this book, which is at once personal and deeply public, you, too, are being inspired to make a movement decision. You could think of it as a sort of civic altar call.

And we don't have to wait for a formal transition to democratic socialism to bring it into existence, in myriad ways, in our communities. In this chapter we'll examine numerous ways to turn the world upside down and create plenty good room for all. Together we can join the faith-filled work of building a multiracial, democratic socialism now. Building a plenty good room movement in our time will require learning from, implementing, and, where needed, editing the lessons left by those who have gone before. Ours is the invitation, and this is the moment.

REMEMBER THAT SOCIALIST PATTERNS ARE WOVEN INTO THE FABRIC OF AMERICA

As we have seen, socialism is not an exotic import, smuggled into the United States generally or plopped into African American communities without any internal reference points. Ella Baker embodied the best of socialist practice through her advocacy for cooperatives, her research with Marvel Cooke on what was once called the Bronx Slave Market, and her consistent model of participatory, class-conscious struggle during the civil rights movement. W. E. B. Du Bois, a cofounder of the NAACP, a staunch socialist, and one-time member of the Communist Party, boldly championed the intersections of pan-Africanism, socialism, and ant-imperialism to such an extent that he died in Ghana, working with Kwame Nkrumah to support that nation's emergent experiment in self-governance. More examples abound, from Episcopal Bishop Theodore Holly and AME Bishop Rev. Reverdy Ransom to movement luminaries like Angela Davis and Alice Walker.

Socialism, moreover, is a deeply embedded thread within the American fabric, especially at the municipal and regional level of governance. Within the energy sector, for example, it is not uncommon for local governments to own and operate the supply of power for entire neighborhoods and regions. Gar Alperowitz, as we noted earlier, wrote an entire book that touches on, among other things, the topic of energy and local public ownership in *What Then Must We Do? Straight Talk about the Next American Revolution*. From the Tennessee Valley Authority in the Southeast to the Long Island Power Authority in the Northeast: we rightly take it for granted that communal or public forms of ownership can deliver reliable energy for businesses, households, and government institutions.

Within the education sector, citizens and residents accept— indeed, *expect*—local government to provide high-quality K–12, community college, and college options for education at low or no cost to students in exchange for taxation. Indeed, most Americans, apart from private schools and the increasingly privatized student loan market, assume that the state is responsible for educating those who live within its jurisdiction.

While we could list further examples from other sectors, the point is clear: Americans, at least since the industrial revolution, are not inherently opposed to removing price as a determining factor in accessing important social goods. Nor are they suspicious of administering systems on a democratic, collective basis. In fact, Americans look to local and regional models of organization to protect and furnish social goods—energy and education, for instance—that are the cornerstones of our life together.

Once we recognize the already existing patterns of socialist and cooperative organization among us, it elevates the political conversation from the fog of passionate, uninformed debate into a more calculating, focused conversation. Which models of organization best advance our freedom, our community interests, and the common good? As soon as we acknowledge that the seeds of socialism are already among us, the question becomes: how do we nurture these seeds in a way that allows for a less anti-Black, more gender-expansive, participatory socialism to expand its presence? What actions must we take to weave patterns of socialism into the fabric of the country, and more critically, throughout all God's creation?

DEBUNK THE MYTH OF MERITOCRACY

A full about-face in our society also involves confronting the dominant ideas of meritocracy. The most subtle and troubling justification for wealth inequality is the false idea of merit-based affluence. This idea essentially means that the astonishingly wealthy have earned the right, by virtue of their asset holdings, to determine that, as of 2023, 37 percent and no higher is the right ceiling for household income taxes. Meritocracy, in everyday terms, holds that uber-rich, well-educated, and high-status individuals are the most qualified to be the referees of what is "good for business" and what constitutes investor confidence. It's a justification for inequality. The ugly implication of meritocracy is that those who are poor are lazy, insufficiently motivated, culturally deficient, or otherwise a problem. The spiritualized version of meritocracy is the prosperity gospel. This kind of misleading, harmful doctrine argues that what separates the rich from the poor, independent of race, gender identity, and country of origin, is that the affluent trust God and work hard for wealth, whereas the poor are presumed to have inadequate levels of work ethic, tolerance for risk taking, and faith in God.

According to the Institute for Policy Studies, which uses the supplemental poverty measure (SPM) rather than the federal poverty measure (which undercounts poverty) to measure poverty, we have 140 million poor and low-wealth individuals in America.[10] The doctrine of meritocracy contends that absolute economic mobility is equally available to everyone and argues that millions are in poverty because of an attitude adjustment challenge. Rather than reckoning with the design flaws of the economy, capitalism trains us to see the prevalence of poverty, unemployment, and economic hardship, and uneven distribution across race and region as a *motivational* deficit. The fact that this myth is hard to detect reflects the ingrained, entrenched, hierarchal nature of our commercial society.

So how do we debunk the myth of meritocracy? One way is to point out that things like the financial position and educational attainment of well-heeled parents and their social networks is often an accurate predictor of the life outcomes of their children. We can reveal the way that wealth and opportunity reproduce themselves, rather than believing that merit is the predictor of life outcomes.

CONFRONT THE CAPITALISM WITHIN

The idea that capitalism exercises a sort of spiritual formation is as old as the insights of Max Weber and as current as the searing analysis of Dr. Keri Day.[11] The spirit that undergirds various capitalisms stunts the development of full and free human spirits and stifles the community-generating presence of the Spirit. The spiritual formation of capitalism reduces moral decisions to cost-benefit calculations and misnames human beings as "human resources." The places where lower-income people of color live, for instance, are not really regarded as communities. They are, instead, seen as "emerging markets," residents of underutilized land, tracts of unrealized profit potential. The nakedness of such ambition is hidden by community benefit agreements, donations to community centers, and worship centers. But the goal is the same: to design the neighborhood in question according to the investment priorities of large-scale commercial enterprises.

There is an emotional and spiritual challenge to the work of bringing about an economic democracy. How do we conduct the inner work of purging, transforming, and shedding our allegiances to and conditioning by capitalist imperialist habits? That work of counter-formation begins with questioning our own interior desires and ingrained patterns of thinking, and working in local communities to divest from the allure of capitalism. This interior, spiritual challenge—of unhooking one's identity from striving and success within a capitalist economy to finding meaning in co-creating a solidarity economy—is a doable yet demanding practice. A capitalist economy requires ever-expanding desires, and imposes a socio-emotional and ideological regime of greed, ambition, and strong preference for purportedly free, unregulated markets. A solidarity economy, on the other hand, requires the ethical practice of applying care to the work of meeting material and cultural human needs. We must learn to build collaboration with the same intensity and skill that engineers use to design and build a bridge. We must put a level of care into resource allocation that matches the collective work of resource generation.

Moving toward a beloved community and a humane economy—one where our legitimate desire for material security does not devolve into a competitive push to dominate other nations, companies, and organizations—will require religious resources. Through prayer, meditation, and casting down the stronghold, we can confront the interior domination of the powers and principalities in our interior lives. We can differentiate between valid desires—to be financially secure, take care of family, and have leisure—and desires for domination and consumerism.

Capitalist, imperialist desires, far too frequently, are embroidered on our hearts. Capitalism has a spiritual formation plan for each of us. The mythology of being a boss, the Instagram profiles of the wealthy, the deification of the private sector as job creators: all these factors condition us to value brand-building and asset-building as the principal aim of a noteworthy life. These factors tilt and lure our hearts to desire things to validate our worth, as signs of how valuable our labor is within the marketplace. By confronting the acquisitive ambitions of capitalist desire within each of us, we can develop the virtues and pleasures of courage and self-examination needed to transform distorted desires for individual gain into the deeper joys of interdependent living on the basis of mutuality and equality.

VALUE THE WORK OF CAREGIVING

The conditions that prompt large-scale organizing, resistance, and theological pushback at the workplace are often mirrored by unjust, stigmatized conditions of work in the home. This type of work, which is traditionally referred to care work—raising children, caring for elders, and attending to loved ones facing illness or recovering from accidents—is usually rendered invisible by a patriarchal, gendered lens. While this kind of work does not always garner a wage, it, too, stands in the crosshairs of a society that rejects the autonomy and dignity of home health aides and other domestic workers.

This situation's shameful contours are illustrated by the fact that as of July 2021, only ten states out of fifty in America had passed a domestic workers' bill of rights.[12] This is actually not a new point. Marxist feminists, womanist theologians, and scholars in related fields—particularly Silvia Federici, bell hooks, Gloria Anzaldúa, among many others—have been making this point for years, arguing for justice in both social reproduction and care, as well as in the production process at out-of-home workplaces. To turn the world upside down, we have to value, legally protect, and assign thriving, family-sustaining wages to all categories of work, regardless of its setting. Domestic workers like house cleaners, home care workers, and nannies deserve the protections, predictable scheduling, and solidarity that other workers receive. Care work, in an equitable economy, merits our attention and protection.

DO THE WORK IN THE CONTEXT OF COMMUNITY

Making a movement decision involves joining, sustaining, or starting organizations that can consolidate our labor, strengthen ecosystems of power, and reinforce our collective yearning for a world beyond the one that we have inherited. Making a movement decision could mean joining groups like the New Economy Coalition and the Public Finance Institute. It might entail joining internationalist groups like the Black Alliance for Peace or Tri-Continental. These organizations may not be household names, but they are posing the critical questions of our moment and attending to issues that ought not be postponed further. Taken together, these organizations point to a possible path beyond racial capitalism's seemingly inevitable regime.

Whatever direction your own movement decision takes, make sure your work draws you toward a collaborative, interdependent project. There is simply no ethically grounded revolution or systems change worthy of the name without deep immersion in, and emergence from, identifiable communities. Labor movements ground themselves in union locals and worker centers. Faith traditions have their communities of practice and spirit. Black communities in the western hemisphere liberated themselves through hush harbors and independent maroon societies of African-descended peoples, some of whom lived alongside Indigenous peoples in places like Jamaica, Haiti, Brazil, and the low country of the United States. Plenty good room movements throughout history require finding common cause with others. Bluntly put: you can't sustainably or effectively work toward plenty good room on your own.

The entry points into what we are calling a plenty good movement are not uniform or one-size-fits-all. For some faith-based community developments corporations, it might mean taking a transformative half step, then full step, toward an economy based on care, human dignity, and reverence for all life. Such a move might entail, in part, pairing equitable real estate development with policy advocacy for anti-displacement zoning and planning policies that place economically vulnerable renters on equal civic footing with homeowners.

For those engaging in direct action and mutual aid, it may look like entering into coalition with those engaging in sectoral bargaining in order to strengthen the decision-making power of workers across industries. The work of the plenty good room movement requires, for everyone, a willingness to be stead-fast, immovable, and abounding in the work of the Lord—not only church work but political work as well. And we must do it together.

GET READY TO BE CHANGED PERSONALLY

There is a personal component to turning the world upside down. In Matthew, Mark, and Luke, Jesus's first words call for a fundamental transformation in the way we think: repent and believe in God's reign. At minimum, this call involves a mindful dedication to letting a sense of the sacred permeate everything we are and all that we do, constantly unlearning, relearning, and studying in a spirit of community, curiosity, and joy.

Choosing a life devoted to changing systems—from capitalism to socialism, from a competitive empire to a cooperative commonwealth, from a scarcity mindset to a worldview of abundance—is bigger than a mere question of ideology and worldview. It is a question of orientation, of one's basic stance in the world. If we are truly "members of one another," as St. Paul maintained in the first century with twenty-first century relevance, change is to be made from within the community, to realize a more just, more equal community.[13]

We can do better than economic models of buying, selling, and distributing that imagine that high-quality food, drinkable water, decent housing and the necessities of abundant life are limited goods. During times of national emergency, like war, a pandemic or a natural disaster, these things can be produced quickly and with tons to spare. But somehow, such goods suddenly become impossible for the government to provide the day after the state of emergency is lifted. We need to turn this conventional form of economic wisdom upside down. As modern monetary theory advocates have argued—including advocates as varied as economists like Stephanie Kelton and pastors like Rev. Dr. Delman Coates—we should take a personal interest in asserting that countries that control their own currency, like the United States, deliver public goods like free healthcare and public education in ways that are mindful of inflation without reinforcing the deficit myth that our national debts necessarily prohibit us from advancing the common good.[14]

In the same spirit that Jeremiah challenged ancient Israel in the eighth century BC to reject a false peace, may we refuse the terms of false peace today. May we carry forward, and innovate within, that prophetic tradition, refusing to settle for the stratification of life chances and instead opting for equitable voice in government and in living conditions. May we say *no* to a system in which people in some communities live a vacation lifestyle every day while others—poor white communities and the majority of Black and blown families—are forced to eke out a life barely resembling survival under soul-fatiguing conditions of inequality. May we regain the capacity to weep with those who weep, grieving and then correcting the conditions that cause cumulative poverty to be the fourth leading cause of death in America.[15]

EXPECT CONFLiCT—AND MANAGE iT TRANSPARENTLY AND EQUiTABLY

Conflict is a built-in, unavoidable dimension of social life. It is also, with sufficient prayer, cooperative effort, and skill, a manageable part of life. It would be beautiful, but untrue, to suggest that building a plenty good room movement means that we arrive at a beloved community without conflict, without polarization. It would be beautiful, and false, to imply that willpower alone makes structural change a reality. We can tell ourselves soothing untruths that help us cope, or we can look reality in the eye. And the reality is that powerful interests prefer that the beloved community remains an intangible, unrealized ideal.

There are, for example, entrenched interests, like for-profit hospitals and insurance companies, that actually *prefer* universal healthcare to be off the table. Elite, gilded interests do not lose sleep over low wages bolstering the annual income statements of multinational corporations. Such organizations recognize that historical, material, and class conflict exists, but they prefer to deny, conceal, or otherwise paper over it. Given the sometimes opaque, sometimes in-your-face realities of class conflict, patriarchy, and geopolitical imbalances of power, the role of both critical media literacy and a free, independent press are musthave components of a plenty good room society. Reliable information and consistent, in-depth coverage of current events are essential inputs for everyday folks to recognize why the odds are stacked against them, as well as who and what is responsible.

Jesus once declared that "in this world, you will have trouble."[16] Translating this into contemporary terms, we could say that this world entails the navigation of love and conflict. The wholesale transformation of a nation's political economy—from finance-driven, tech-dominated, speculative real-estate capitalism to a historically informed and spiritually grounded democratic socialism—takes consistent collaboration, creative visioning, and a willingness to enter into debate and political contest. We can do all this without being needlessly dogmatic, sectarian, or demonizing.

Conflict need not be romanticized, but neither should politeness, decorum, and adherence to protocol. The sacrosanct status of "civility" is proven to exist by the hand wringing that follows the slightest hint of class conflict in federal, state, and local politics. When the siren song of profit maximization arises at Amazon, or when Walmart translates the humanity of people into a budget line item—like input expenses, costs of goods sold, or production costs—we have a problem. That problem exceeds piecemeal solutions, and it should exceed any desire on our part to be merely polite. We have a problem that calls on all of us to be moral engineers, persons unafraid to articulate how and why we need to design laws, organizational models, campaigns, and movements that work for those whom Frantz Fanon called the "wretched of the earth." We need to envision models of social enterprise that are truly equitable and non-exploitative. And we need to demand them now.

LOOK TO THE PAST FOR LESSONS FOR THE FUTURE

We need not look far for examples of principled politics that helped to turn the world upside down. For instance, we can look to Rev. Dr. Martin King's insistence on militant nonviolence, call for a guaranteed annual income, and support for labor unions, including the National Welfare Rights Union, that helped to bring about the Poor People's Campaign. As noted earlier in this chapter, we can look at Ella Jo Baker's community-grounded research in the Bronx Slave Market and organizing of cooperatives as part of the Young Negro Cooperatives League during the Great Depression. We can also look at the full career arc of Asa Phillip Randolph, the storied labor union organizer, publisher, and social movement architect. That vocation began with his socialist organizing in Harlem, where he co-launched an outlet called the Messenger, and continued into his later initiation of the direct action in the March to Washington movement. Additionally, his legacy of building a constitutionally informed politics of strike, mass demonstration, public goods, and freedom budget illustrate what it might look like to move our already mixed economy in the direction of a culturally inclusive, economic democracy. These illustrations are snapshots of a larger tradition of democratic socialism and grassroots promotion of commonwealth economies.

How else might we convert our ideals into institutions capable of implementing what we dream about, pray about, plan about, and fight for? One way is to excavate little-known histories and arguments concerning American cooperative work. The Black radical diaspora contains countless examples that can inform the work to build a plenty good room movement. As a Black Christian preacher committed to socialism, I recall the legacies of Angela Davis and Rev. Dr. Martin Luther King, emerging outlets like the Hampton Institute, Prism Reports, and *Jacobin* magazine; veteran groups like Democratic Socialists of America, the Movement for Black Lives, and the Institute for Policy Studies. I recall the early 1930s poetry of Langston Hughes calling for a socialist political order; magazines like *Freedomways*, a Black political and cultural journal that ran from the 1960s through the 1980s; and the recent launch of *Hammer and Hope*, a Black studies popular journal of politics arguing for a different approach for, among other things, economic democracy. One might lift up the speeches of Malcolm X and the Rainbow Coalition of Fred Hampton in the Black Panther Party of Chicago, the scholarship and guerilla intellectual work of Dr. Charisse Burden-Stelly and her conceptually clear insights on super exploitation and triple oppression. Additional examples include socialists and revolutionary individuals of faith like Julius Nyerere, a revolutionary Catholic leader who successfully led Tanzania to independence from British colonialism, and Episcopalian bishop Theodore Holly, stationed in Haiti, who recognized the conflict between industrial society and the principles of love that we might name as "universal kinship."

Remembering this contemporary work and its precedents gives us the courage, inspiration, and defiant confidence in the face of systems seeking to bully us into silence and falling in line with the status quo. Once such works of remembrance renew our minds and steel our determination, we can then strategize and contradict the common sense of our time in the name of a more humane, more holy way of organizing our society.

MOVE TOWARD A SOLiDARiTY ECONOMY

We can advance economic justice by making indivisible, culturally affirming, faith-rooted moves toward solidarity economies. In the context of Black churches, whose particular stories hold universal importance, a movement toward a more equitable economy can help promote a consensus-based society of fellowship and fairness, based in the fullness inherent with God's creation. We can migrate toward a solidarity economy through connecting congregations with community-based groups looking to interrupt predatory economies and reverse gentrification by establishing community land trusts and cooperative housing. Credit unions are another example prevalent in many Black churches. Credit unions are member-based financial institutions that provide below-market loans for mortgages, consumer items, and other conventional uses. Through pooling the resources of members, credit unions create a financial service that meets the immediate needs of members while also enabling them to withdraw participation in, and allegiance to, a predatory financial system. That system of traditional banking, which brought down the entire economy in the 2008 recession through its packaging and selling of collateralized debt obligations, is a system that could cost us not only our money but also our souls.

We must continue to try to alleviate human suffering through direct service and mutual aid, such as creating community fridges, convening a people's library, and creating pooled funding to meet unmet needs. But meeting individual needs alone, with no further acts of liberation, is insufficient. Community development is likewise critical, but it, too, is inadequate to meet the full range of human and environmental needs by itself. Better still is organizing and policy advocacy for living wages, better benefits, and affordable housing; despite their undeniable value, these works are also not enough to meet our complex needs on a solitary basis. All these approaches are essential parts of a larger, social change strategy that redresses and repairs the material *and* moral injuries of racial capitalism, gender injustice, and imperialism. Socialist approaches strike at the root cause of exploitation by using regulation, strikes, legislation, and cooperative production across private and public industry to curtail corporate influence, expand worker power, and increase the standard of living in lower-income communities.

MOVE FROM RELIGIOUS CENTRISM TO TRANSFORMATIVE FAITH

In the United States and in far too many industrialized nations, Christianity has become basically a synonym for white political conservatism, authoritarian governments, and color-blind theology that throws holy water on top of structural racism, nativist laws and curriculum, and gender discrimination. We must make clear that God doesn't endorse a top-down economy that clusters the hardest, most undesirable work on the tired shoulders and feet of vulnerable people. We must challenge dominant cultures to convert to a spirit of mutuality in wielding power, and invite communities of faith and ethical ambition to join an ever-expanding fellowship of humanity seeking to do justice, love mercy, and walk humbly with God. In addition to moral suasion, the influence of the law, energized and informed social movements, and equitably administered public policy remains critically important for ensuring that justice happens according to civil right and social guarantees, rather than resting predominantly on the whim and volition of the powerful.

While conservative religion presents its share of challenges, it is also the case that progressive religion, in a similar yet distinct way, faces its own set of conundrums. For instance, conventional religious progressivism often seeks to promote gradualist, issue-specific visions of equity rather than actionable, system-wide ideals of economic justice with a sense of moral urgency. We must walk toward transformative faith in a socialist register, one that holds governments, corporations, and all organizations accountable to Black folks. We can do this through models like co-determination and unionization, worker power, a humane labor process, and ecologically responsible operations. This approach assumes that prophetic voices of faith-filled socialism, when acting independently of our two-party system, can dream of and enact more just policies such as social housing and land banks instead of displacement-based housing; worker co-ops and day laborer initiatives instead of simply living wages; credit unions and sovereign wealth funds instead of simply breaking up big banks.

Articulating a socialism of beloved community also provides religious folks and people of conscience with a consistent storyline of economic justice. Absent socialism or something analogous, religious centrists and progressives may unintentionally preach a Beloved Community that generally resembles Democratic Party talking points, rather than pushing the policy agenda of mainstream parties and third parties toward a fuller vision of justice and plenty good room. Religious progressivism, despite the best of intentions, can fall prey to a parochial American view of what justice, liberty, and *e pluribus unum* mean. For all the virtues of the tradition, it rarely addresses economic sources of capital accumulation and labor exploitation and the disparate harms it imposes across the lived experiences of race, gender, place, and immigration status. If the goal is to co-create liberation, are we not morally obligated to build toward a world beyond the lethal inequality management of capitalism?

Turning the world upside down is an urgent call of faith, one that emerges from our conscience, one that inspires us thorough careful, consistent study of history, and one that beckons us forward. Turning upside down the world of imperialism, capitalism, and heteropatriarchy, as the best of the Jesus movement has long sought to do, involves further steps. We'll return to some of these ideas at a later point about recognizing the spiritual dimensions of this work.

BUILD NETWORKS OF POPULAR DEMOCRACY

Rebuilding Black worker associations and labor union movements at the national, state, and local levels is a necessary step that positions workers to defend their interests independent of the performance and ideology of political parties. Without well-organized worker centers or membership-based unions fighting for wages, fair scheduling, decent benefits—as well as the common good of non-members—Black economic futures will remain stuck in a cycle of what community organizer and social entrepreneur Jamye Wooten calls "re-activism," as illustrated in his remarks: "Hashtags based campaigns or decentralized movements without a holistic ideological framework keep us in reactivism mode, moving from issue to issue, leaving little energy to organize for sustainable solutions and change." The antidote to this, Wooten argues, is to build campaigns with a holistic ideological framework and well-networked institutions, which can help move us #BeyondreActivism.[17]

The work of popular democracy, housed in communities, can happen right alongside representative democracy, housed in the government. Popular democracy can reclaim the ideal of democracy from being merely a word used by both parties to whip up fear during election season. Instead, popular democracy offers actionable inspiration for bandaging the wounds caused by racial capitalism and working to replace the system altogether.

There's a reason that the Service Employees International Union (SEIU) has long waged a Fight for $15 an Hour and a Union—a major part of that reason is to help establish a popular democracy that relies on expert knowledge without ignoring or devaluing the role of experiential knowledge in fostering sustained action for justice work. SEIU's Fight for $15 campaign remains an instructive effort, even as the cost of living has long outpaced the initial courage and necessity of that transformative demand. Living-wage employment, plainly put, is a public good that should be equally available to everyone. In fact, we could call for a social wage, as much of the political science literature maintains, that returns wrongly captured financial value and community public goods back to a multiracial, cross-generational working class. Networks of popular democracy, in so many ways, are essential for making this type of change happen.

MAKE ART, CREATE CULTURE

Turning the world upside down also involves using arts, culture, and creative initiatives to dismantle socioeconomic racism. This is the lesson of Emory Douglas, the artist who crafted and created much of the work for the Black Panther Party for Self-Defense in the 1960s. Douglas' work represents art that simultaneously informs Black audiences, uplifts them, and points out ways to abolish the conditions that generate preventable pain and suffering in our communities. Similar to Douglas' work, podcasts and informative shows like Faith and Capital, Magnificast, and IMixWhatILike epitomize the best of popular education, alerting viewers and participants to the full measure of their collective self-efficacy as citizens, organizers, and moral engineers whose design thinking can help turn the world upside down and make it right side up.

Stories, sermons, songs, street art, documentaries, children's books, op-eds, and other cultural productions are foundational, not peripheral, to the work of dismantling the imprint of socioeconomic racism within our minds, theologies, and politics. Socioeconomic narratives baptized in racism—which make poverty seem like a moral failure rather than a policy failure—must be identified and replaced with new narratives that are as healing as they are enjoyable. The ideological impact of socioeconomic racism—which makes capitalism seem like a natural, immutable, and commonsense reality—is precisely what must be demystified and refuted. It must be replaced with a new conventional wisdom, one rooted in the hearts and minds of working people, our culture, and our shared environment while remaining open to further reasoning and deliberation.

SUPPORT FREEDOM OF THE PRESS, CIVIL LIBERTIES, AND LOCAL POLITICS

Any socialism worthy of the name requires a deep commitment to a free, independent press and civil liberties. These liberties include freedom of assembly, freedom of speech, freedom of religion, and all the attendant anti-discrimination provisions outlined in legislation like the Civil Rights Act of 1866 and the Civil Rights Act of 1964.

With such freedoms in place and vigorously upheld, a participatory socialism invites ordinary citizens to engage in a dual process: first, evaluating the prevailing institutional arrangements of a city or town's status quo from the vantage point of justice, freedom, and a sense of kinship among humanity. Second, and equally important, is the effort to craft a better future from local legislative seats, appointed positions, neighborhood advisory bodies, school board offices, and executive posts like a mayoralty or county commissioner roles. Such work can be hidden and have low visibility, but local governments provide critical services and augment the critical but smaller-scale work of community-based organizations. Restoring public confidence in local administrative and electoral politics means offering a bold alternative to the status quo in what shared governance can entail. When they work in concert with rather than in opposition to each other, imagine what local government, civically engaged networks and groups, social movements, and community-centered commerce, like credit unions and public banks, can protect and provide.

RECOGNIZE THE SPIRITUAL DIMENSIONS OF THE WORK

Racialized capitalism is an environment within which all other social injustices take place. Each social experience of evil—the hostile, interlocking systems of the powers and principalities that Delores Williams calls the "demonarchy"—must be dealt with.[18] There can be no generic, boilerplate casting out of demons—it must happen by name, articulating the phenomena that harm God's people.

As an example of how racial capitalism blankets injustices, a cursory review of some of society's most infamous injustices will suffice. Think of the thirteenth amendment, with its carveout for incarcerated servitude that encouraged convict leasing and prison labor camps in the nineteenth century. Recall the anti-Black bargaining chip of the New Deal, which secured historic protections for white laborers at the expensive social cost of leaving agriculture and domestic work—the industries where most Black folks were employed—without laws to shield them from southern white patriarchy and racism. Racial capitalism, in a theological sense, can be seen as one of the elemental spirits of this present age, to invoke the symbols of the New Testament, that identify how larger-than-human forces oppress and subjugate our species. Turning the world upside down for Jesus and justice, then, requires a faithful naming of and reckoning with racism-meets-capitalism.

One point that is important to note here: other faith and ethical traditions will draw on their own histories, symbols, and narratives for naming. This is appropriate and to be expected in a society that deeply values the first-amendment rights of religious freedom. A vibrant, critically thinking Christian is least in danger of withering away when they recognize and graciously engage with people of differing religious, ideological, and ethical traditions.

Racial capitalism also undermines the church's communal witness by being hostile to Christian traditions: traditions like being on guard against greed, doing justice and loving people with mercy, taking care of the least of these, practicing cooperative economics, and doing what the apostle Paul calls remembering the poor. Capitalism, in its global and US contexts, is a social order of stratification and domination, an upward clustering of financial value and wealth, and a continual scouring of the earth for workforces to exploit and for communities to convert into revenue-generating, market opportunities.

In Dutch South Africa, extremely racialized capitalism was justified by a doctrine called "the order of creation," which held that God establishes whites to rule and Blacks to serve as an explanation for how the state-sponsored segregation of apartheid can be seen as compatible with God's agenda. Such doctrines, stripped of formal expression, attempt to pour honey on the harsh edges of racial domination with a false promise and presentation of Christianity, in order to give inhumane regimes the appearance of moral legitimacy.

Given these false claims, it's important for Christians to push *back* against misleading moral narratives, and push *for* a just, structural transformation of our economic and political system.

What does it look like to embark on—or continue—this kind of justice work? In some measure, it looks like political education that prioritizes community organizing, voter outreach and mobilization, messaging work through media, and advocacy campaigns on specific issues. Early in my calling, I established a social justice ministry at the Greater Allen A.M.E. Cathedral of New York, a megachurch in New York City. Through that work, I helped mobilize a team of church and community members to serve in all of the foregoing areas and have found them to be useful entry points into effective ministry and a more holistic view of God co-working with humanity in the world. In settings across the country and throughout the world, congregational alliances with issue-based advocates and trusted community-rooted organizations can be powerful coalitions. Together, drawing on our religious and spiritual identities, we can create experiments in disrupting scarcity and moving toward a socialist, humane economy. We can create spaces where plenty good room abounds.

BUILDING A PLENTY GOOD ROOM MOVEMENT

We can turn the world upside down for justice by combining our resources and relationships in countless ways—some better than others. If we choose a more efficient, excellent, and equitable way, we can partner with God in setting right the wrongdoing of the world, and in the process, institutionalize a sacred truth: there is plenty good room for all of God's children to thrive.

Some of us may build toward a plenty good room world by co-curating a solidarity economy that favors smaller-scale interventions, regionally grounded economies, and elevating the role of planning and equity in our macroeconomy. Others may write op-eds, preach, teach, and create the narrative conditions for envisioning and desiring a world beyond the advertisement-soaked, algorithm-laced spectacle that we have. Such work, as we discussed earlier, is the complex task of embodying and articulating freedom dreams.

Some persons and networks will prefer conventional forms of politics: lobbying legislative committees, urging government agencies to implement policies that benefit working people, supporting principled elected officials for office—with all the attendant limits and opportunities. We might imagine congregations, labor unions, and community-centered commerce intervening directly in the economy through agitation and redistribution: organizing boycotts and divestment campaigns; supporting workers on strike for better wages, working conditions, and decision-making power. Certainly, in the wake of the Covid-19 pandemic, we witnessed—and will continue to witness—the distribution of mutual aid funds to those with unmet needs.

Here's the take-home point: building a plenty good room movement will require all sorts of people to do all sorts of tasks. We can all identify how the contributions in our corner of the world can add up to transformed societies and renewed minds, where neither whiteness nor capital is supreme.

Co-creating an economy of enough for all is our honor and our obligation. It is what we, the living, owe the ancestors before us, the God abiding with us, and the young who will walk beside us.

EPILOGUE
PRAYING WITHOUT CEASING

The twentieth-century mystic Howard Washington Thurman once wrote: "Prayer grows out of an imperative urgency, sometimes pointed, sometimes diffused. It enables one to keep fresh and focused in spirit the dedication to which one's life is given. Again and again, it creates a profound sense of power deep within the mind, expressing itself in strange new courage and purposefulness."[1]

Praying without ceasing is an ethic of life and of faith. It flows from the recognition of what Thurman calls an "imperative urgency," one expressing itself "in strange new courage and purposefulness."[2] We are the ones capable of embodying and building societies that approximate good news to the poor in the mood and spirit of prayer.

Our attempts at building an inclusive, anti-imperial, and reparative democratic socialism, which we have detailed in this book, constitute an embodied prayer. Embodied prayer includes eyes-closed and fingers-interlocked petitions, but it goes beyond that style too. Embodied prayer is a sacred *and* political exercise of pursuing racial justice and gender equity by working to establish an economic democracy through policy advocacy and implementation, through cooperative enterprise, and through political and religious education that identifies and redresses the root causes of our suffering.

Thurman once argued that whatever blocks one from experiencing a sense of connection with God is an obstacle that must be brought low and removed. In that way, the channel and flow between God's spirit and our own might be restored. His words are lamentably gendered on this point, but hopefully we can hear him speaking to all persons in this insight: "For the mystic, social action is sacramental, because it is not an end in itself. Always, it is the individual who must be addressed, located and released, underneath his misery and his hunger and his destitution. That whatever may be blocking his way to his own center where his altar may be found, this must be removed."[3]

The commitment to socialism of the sort that we have been considering involves a retrieval of what Thurman notes here as a sacramental, altar-oriented approach to decisive action. Racial capitalism—and its cousins of empire, patriarchy, and me-first religion—is an obstacle to accessing the altar that Thurman names. Racial capitalism, and all the oppressions that bear family resemblance to it, are spiritual and psychological threats in addition to economic and political threats. They impede the cultivation of vibrant, interior lives that are hidden with God. All oppressions block our partnership with the Divine to work toward fuller visions of liberation, abundant life, and an ever-expanding vision of the common good.

For example: the massive deforestation of American cities and the emission of greenhouse gases not only threatens our climate and pollutes our air, it can also make communities feel like their prayers for "the heavens to declare the glory of God" are going unanswered, unheeded, and utterly disregarded by human beings made in that same God's image and likeness.[4] Reestablishing the beauty of the earth—as faith traditions and cultures the world over have long recognized—is equally a matter of what humanitarian and New Testament scholar Albert Schweitzer called "reverence for life" and of implementing the ideals of love and justice that can lead us to a more equitable planet and society.

Prayer is an anointing that reinforces our determination to work for distributive justice, for an enriching culture where white supremacy is defeated and the dignity of all God's people is seen and savored. For such prayer to be inclusive rather than artificial, it must reach across the cleavages of class oppression, gender inequity, nation-state borders, and structural racism.

There is, I believe, plenty good room in God's creation for a world where an inclusive economics serves people, planet, and our deepest principles. And to the extent that we both believe and harbor unbelief at once, let us resolve—with a holy stubbornness and solidarity—to try the great task of building a people-centered, spiritually rooted socialism. If we fail, let us fail in the right direction. If we aren't confident that it will work, let us try anyhow. In the sable wisdom of Black churches in the United States, we can run on and see what the end will be.

I leave you with a prayer, a benedictory poem. It is a summons to attempt what our hearts know must be attempted, informed by faith, research, logic, and imagination. Why conclude with a poem? A truism of politics is that campaigning happens in poetry and governing happens in prose. It is fitting to issue a concluding call to action in poetry so that, together, we might do the prose-oriented work of building a world of plenty good room for all God's children.

TRY ANYHOW

Racial justice is a worthwhile ideal
But unworkable in America
Or any other nation state,
According to some.

Socialism is a beautiful dream
But impossible to realize,
According to some.

Ending patriarchy in our generation
Is a deeply ethical goal
But unable to be dragged into today,
According to some.

Perhaps they are right.
But so is the dream.

For the sake of its embodiment.
For our elders, children, and those in between.
Let us try anyhow.
And see what the end will be!

NOTES

INTRODUCTION

1 Talmon Joseph Smith and Karl Russell, "The Greatest Wealth Transfer in History Is Here, With Familiar (Rich) Winners," *New York Times*, May 14, 2023, https://www.nytimes.com/2023/05/14/business/economy/wealth-generations.html.

2 Irving Dilliard, *Mr. Justice Brandeis, Great American: Press Opinion and Public Appraisal* (St. Louis, MO: Modern View Press, 1941).

3 Matthew 6:24, King James Version.

4 Luke 1:46–55.

5 Alison P. Guise Johnson, "Redeeming Black Survival," in *Walking through the Valley: Womanist Explorations in the Spirit of Katie Geneva Cannon*, ed. Emilie M. Townes et al. (Louisville, KY: Westminster John Knox, 2022), 54.

6 Gary Dorrien, "Rediscovering the Black Social Gospel," *Harvard Divinity Bulletin*, Summer/Autumn 2015, https://bulletin.hds.harvard.edu/recovering-the-black-social-gospel/.

7 Luke 4:18–20, NRSV; Galatians 2:10, NRSV.

8 OutKast, "Elevators (Me and You)," LaFace Records, 1996. (ADD recording date and where accessed (CD, Spotify, etc – see CMOS 14.263 for examples)

9 Ruth Wilson Gilmore, "Abolition Geography and the Problem of Innocence," in *Futures of Black Radicalism*, ed. Gaye Theresa Johnson and Alex Lubin (New York: Verso Books, 2017), 225–48.

10 Oshan Jarow, "Poverty is a major public health crisis. Let's treat it like one," *Vox*, June 14, 2023, https://www.vox.com/

future-perfect/23792854/poverty-mortality-study-public-health-antipoverty-america-deaths-poor-life-expectancy.

11 2 Thessalonians 3:10, NRSV; Matthew 26:11, NRSV.

12 "International Covenant on Economic, Social, and Cultural Rights," United Nations Treaty Collection, New York, December 16, 1966, https://treaties.un.org/Pages/ViewDetails.aspx?src=IND&mtdsg_no=IV-3&chapter=4&clang=_en.

13 For a general overview, see C. Wann Woodward, *The Strange Career of Jim Crow* (New York: Oxford University Press, 1955), and Douglas Blackmon, *Slavery by Another Name: The Re-Enslavement of Black Americans from the Civil War to World War II* (New York: Anchor Books, 2008).

14 William Sloane Coffin, *Credo* (Louisville, KY: Westminster John Knox Press, 2004).

15 International Work Group for Indigenous Affairs, "Reconciliation between Germany and Namibia: towards reparation for the first genocide of the 20th century," October 12, 2021, https://tinyurl.com/3wywcty9.

16 bell hooks, *Ain't I a Woman? Black Women and Feminism* (London: Pluto Press, 1982).

CHAPTER 1

1 bell hooks, *Belonging: A Culture of Place* (New York: Routledge, 2008), 5.

2 hooks, *Belonging*, 5.

3 Peter Marcuse and David Madden, *In Defense of Housing* (Brooklyn: Verso, 2016), 127–128.

4 For more on racial capitalism, see Cedric J. Robinson, *Black Marxism: The Making of the Black Radical Tradition* (Chapel Hill, NC: University of North Carolina Press, 1983).

5 Ruth Wilson Gilmore, *Change Everything: Racial Capitalism and the Case for Abolition* (Chicago: Haymarket Books, 2021).

6 For more on this theory, see David Harvey, "The Right to City," *International Journal of Urban and Regional Research* 27, no. 4 (December 2003): 939–941. https://doi.org/10.1111/j.0309-1317.2003.00492.x.

7 Anna Domaradzka, "Urban Social Movements and the Right to the City: An Introduction to the Special Issue on Urban Mobilization," *VOLUNTAS: International Journal of Voluntary and Nonprofit Organizations* 29 (August 20, 2018), 607–620. https://doi.org/10.1007/s11266-018-0030-y.

8 Marlena Jackson-Retondo and Alexis Madrigal, "Historian Keeanga-Yamahtta Taylor on the Racial Wealth Gap and the Crisis of American Capitalism," *KQED*, November 10, 2021, https://www.kqed.org/news/11893704/historian-keeanga-yamahtta-taylor-on-the-racial-wealth-gap-and-the-crisis-of-american-capitalism.

9 A recurring theme in Scripture, see, for example: 1 Kings 4:25: Micah 4:4.

10 Todd Swanstrom, "The Nonprofitization of United States Housing Policy: Dilemmas of Community Development," in "Community Development in the United States," special issue, *Community Development Journal* 34, no. 1 (January 1999): 28–37.

11 "July 19, 1881: Atlanta Washerwomen's Strike," Zinn Education Project: Teaching People's History, https://www.zinnedproject.org/news/tdih/atlanta-washerwomens-strike-reconstruction.

12 Atlanta Tribune, The Magazine, "The Atlanta Washerwomen Strike of 1881," https://atlantatribune.com/tag/washerwoman-strike/; see also Tera Hunter, *To Joy My Freedom: Southern Black Women's Lives and Labors After the Civil War* (Cambridge: Harvard Press: 1997).

13 AFL-CIO. "Atlanta's Washerwomen Strike," https://aflcio.org/about/history/labor-history-events/atlanta-washerwomen-strike.

14 Karl Marx, "The Eighteenth Brumaire of Louis Bonaparte," *Die Revolution*, 1852.

15 Heather McGhee, "Introduction," in *The Sum of Us: What Racism costs Everyone and How We can Prosper Together* (New York: Penguin Random House, 2021), xi.

16 Martin Luther King Jr., "Where Do We Go From Here?" Stanford University: The Martin Luther King Jr. Research and Education Institute, August 16, 1967, https://kinginstitute.stanford.edu/where-do-we-go-here.

17 Josh Green. "How the Cascade Heights 'Revolution' Transformed Atlanta," *Curbed Atlanta*, September 23, 2015, https://atlanta.curbed.com/2015/9/23/9918262/how-the-cascade-heights-revolution-transformed-atlanta.

18 For more, see Peter Marcuse and David Madden, *In Defense of Housing: The Politics of Crisis* (Brooklyn: Verso Books, 2016); and Keenanga-Yamahtta Taylor, *From #BlackLivesMatter to Black Liberation* (Chicago: Haymarket Books, 2016).

19 National Low-Income Housing Coalition, "Out of reach 2023: The high cost of housing," NLHIC press release, June 14, 2023, https://nlihc.org/resource/nlihc-releases-out-reach-2023-high-cost-housing.

20 Goodie Mob, an Atlanta-based group of hip-hop artists, popularized this term on their debut album, *Soul Food*.

21 Teresa Wiltz, "How Atlanta Became a City I Barely Recognize," *Politico* Magazine, September 16, 2022, https://www.politico.com/news/magazine/2022/09/16/atlanta-black-mecca-inequality-00055390.

22 The Associated Press, "Evanston, Illinois, becomes first U.S. city to pay reparations to Black residents." *NBC News*, March, 23, 2021, https://www.nbcnews.com/news/us-news/evanston-illinois-becomes-first-u-s-city-pay-reparations-blacks-n1261791; see also, National African-American Reparations Commission, "First 16 participants of Evanston's historic Local Reparations Restorative Housing Program select benefits," Reparation News and Views, May 4, 2022, https://reparationscomm.org/reparations-news/first-partici pants-evanstons-local-reparations-restorative-housing-program/.

23 For more on this theme, see Matthew Desmond, *Poverty, by America* (New York: Crown Publishing Group, 2023).

24 Thomas Wheatley, "Fighting for Density in the Nation's Sprawl Capital," *Next City*, June 4, 2012, https://nextcity.org/features/atlanta-sprawl-planning-density-sunbelt-cities; see also Christopher Famighetti and Darrick Hamilton, "The Great Recession, education, race, and homeownership," *Economic Policy Institute* (Working Economics Blog), May 15, 2019, https://www.epi.org/blog/the-great-recession-education-race-and-homeownership/.

25 Bill Chappell, "Shake Shack Returns $10 Million Loan To U.S. Program For Small Businesses," *NPR*, April 20, 2020, https://www.npr.org/sections/coronavirus-live-updates/2020/04/20/838439215/shake-shack-returns-10-million-loan-to-u-s-program-for-small-businesses.

26 Gustavo Gutierrez, *A Theology of Liberation: History, Politics, and Salvation* (Maryknoll, NY: Orbis Books, 1971).

CHAPTER 2

1 For more on this theme, see Ibram H. Rogers (later Ibram X. Kendi), *The Black Campus Movement: Black Students and the Racial Reconstitution of Higher Education, 1965–1972* (New York: Palgrave Macmillan, 2012).

2 Abraham Heschel, *God In Search of Man* (New York: Farrar, Straus, and Giroux, 1976); See also Bhaskar Sunkara, *The Socialist Manifesto: The Case for Radical Politics in an Age of Extreme Inequality* (New York: Basic Books, 2019).

3 Barbara A. Holmes, *Joy Unspeakable: Contemplative Practices of the Black Church*, 2nd edition (Minneapolis, MN: Fortress Press, 2017).

4 Psalm 46:10.

5 Susannah Heschel, "Their Feet Were Praying," Jewish Telegraphic Agency, January 10, 2012, https://www.jta.org/2012/01/10/ny/their-feet-were-praying.

6 Noah Adams, "The Inspiring Force of 'We Shall Overcome,'" All Things Considered, *NPR*, August 28, 2013, https://www.npr.org/2013/08/28/216482943/the-inspiring-force-of-we-shall-overcome.

7 Ephesians 6:12, KJV.

8 Jean-Jacques Rousseau, *Of the Social Contract and Other Political Writings* (London: Penguin Publishing Group, 2012). Originally published in 1762.

9 For more on this theme, see Nikki M. Taylor, *America's First Black Socialist: The Radical Life of Peter H. Clark* (Lexington, KY: University Press of Kentucky, 2013).

10 Nina Simone, "I Wish I Knew How It Would Feel To Be Free," *Silk & Soul*, RCA, October 1967.

11 Jaime Lowe, "What Does California Owe Its Incarcerated Firefighters?" *Atlantic*, July 27, 2021, https://www.theatlantic.com/politics/archive/2021/07/california-inmate-firefighters/619567/.

12 For more on this topic, see Manning Marable, *Race, Reform, and Rebellion: The Second Reconstruction and Beyond in Black America, 1945–2006*, 3rd ed. (Jackson, MS: University Press of Mississippi, 2007).

13 Joel 2:28.

14 For a deeper dive, see Peter Paris, *The Social Teaching of Black Churches* (Minneapolis, MN: Fortress Press, 1985).

15 Gayraud S. Wilmore, *Black Religion and Black Radicalism: An Interpretation of the Religious History of African Americans* (New York: Anchor Press, 1973).

16 Galatians 1:6.

17 2 Timothy 4:7–8.

18 Gustavo Gutierrez, *We Drink from Our Own Wells: The Spiritual Journey of a People* (Maryknoll, NY: Orbis Books: 1983), 127, 131.

19 Habakkuk 2:2.

20 Frederick Douglass, "West India Emancipation," (speech, Canandaigua, New York, August 3, 1857), retrieved from University of Rochester Frederick Douglass Project, https://rbscp.lib.rochester.edu/4398.

21 Kendall Glynn, "Atlanta workers at Starbucks, Amazon, and Delta shook things up in 2022," *Atlanta Civic Circle*, January 5, 2023, https://atlantaciviccircle.org/2023/01/05/2022-labor-recap/.

22 Haley Ott, "Strike in U.K. sees up to half a million workers walk off jobs in biggest industrial action in over a decade," *CBS News*, February 1, 2023, https://www.cbsnews.com/news/strike-in-uk-general-strike-teacher-rail-transport-industrial-action/.

23 Matthew 6:24.

CHAPTER 3

1 Heather McGhee, *The Sum of Us*.

2 Heather McGhee, *The Sum of Us*, 364.

3 E. E. Schattschneider, *Semi-Sovereign People* (New York: Holt, 1960), 35.

4 Heather McGhee, "Never a Real Democracy," *The Sum of Us*, 161.

5 Max Weber, *Economy and Society: An outline of interpretive sociology*, vols. 1–2, eds. G. Roth & C. Wittich (Berkeley: University of California Press, 1978). (Original work published 1921).

6 Karl Evers-Hillstrom, "State of Money in Politics: The price of victory is steep," *Open Secrets*, February 19, 2019, https://www.opensecrets.org/news/2019/02/state-of-money-in-politics-the-price-of-victory-is-steep/.

7 Participatory Budgeting Project. "Impacts," https://www.participatorybudgeting.org/impacts/.

8 Grace Del Vecchio, "Here's what you need to know about participatory budgeting," *Chicago Reader*, April 30, 2021, https://chicagoreader.com/news-politics/heres-what-you-need-to-know-about-participatory-budgeting/.

9 "Our Mission: Regional Solidarity Economies," New Economy Coalition website, https://neweconomy.net/about/#mission-vision.

10 International Labour Organization, "Social and Solidarity Economy."

11 "Our Vision: We Envision a World . . . ," New Economy Coalition website, https://neweconomy.net/about/.

12 William J. Barber II, "Every Crucifixion Needs a Witness," *Boston Review*, May 28, 2019, https://www.bostonreview.net/articles/toussaint-losier-william-j-barber-ii-every-crucifixion-needs-witness/.

13 Zeynep Tufekci, "Do Protests Even Work?" *Atlantic*, June 24, 2020, https://www.theatlantic.com/technology/archive/2020/06/why-protests-work/613420/.

14 Adam Clayton Powell, "Black Power In The Church," *The Black Scholar* 2, no. 4 (December 1970): 32–34.

15 Walter Brueggemann, quote found in William Sloane Coffin's *A Passion for the Possible* (Louisville, KY: Westminster John Knox Press, 1993), 34.

16 SNCC Digital Gateway, "Fannie Lou Hamer Founds Freedom Farm Cooperative," https://snccdigital.org/events/fannie-lou-hamer-founds-freedom-farm-cooperative/.

17 SNCC Digital Gateway, "Fannie Lou Hamer."

18 The Transnational Institute, "About," https://www.tni.org/en/about. For more on this theme, see The Transnational Institute, "Public Finance For the Future We Want," June 24, 2019, https://www.tni.org/en/publication/public-finance-for-the-future-we-want.

19 Psalm 24:1.

20 Marx/Engels Selected Works, Volume Three, *Critique of the Gotha Programme*, 13–30.

CHAPTER 4

1 Pew Research Center, "Modest Declines in Positive Views of 'Socialism' and 'Capitalism' in U.S.," September 19, 2022, https://www.pewresearch.org/politics/2022/09/19/modest-declines-in-positive-views-of-socialism-and-capitalism-in-u-s/.

2 Rachel Treisman, "Essential Workers Hold Walkouts and Protests in 'National Strike for Black Lives.'" NPR. July 20, 2020.

https://www.npr.org/sections/live-updates-protests-for-racial-justice/2020/07/20/893316011/essential-workers-hold-walk outs-and-protests-in-national-strike-for-black-lives. Accessed on October 1, 2023.

3 Cornel West, "The Witness," *Black Theology and Socialist Thought* 63, no. 4 (April 1980): 16–19.

4 West, "The Witness."

5 Amaryah Armstrong, *Christian Order and Racial Order: What Cedric Robinson Can Teach Us.* The Bias. https://www.christiansocialism.com/2020/06/03/cedric-robinson-racial-order-christianity-socialism/. June 3, 2020. Accessed on October 1, 2023.

6 Luke 4:18–20.

7 Martin Luther King Jr., "To Coretta Scott," Stanford University, The Martin Luther King Jr. Research and Education Institute, July 18, 1952.

8 Martin Luther King Jr. *"Thou, Dear God": Prayers That Open Hearts and Spirits*, ed. Lewis V. Baldwin (Boston: Beacon Press, 2014).

9 Michael Harrington, *The Other America* (New York: Macmillan Publishing Company, 1962).

10 Martin Luther King, "I Have a Dream," University of Minnesota Human Rights Library, August 28, 1963, Retrieved from: http://hrlibrary.umn.edu/education/lutherspeech.html.

11 For more on this theme, see Walter Wink, *Engaging the Powers: Engagement and Resistance in a World of Domination* (Minneapolis, MN: Fortress Press, 1992).

12 Emilie Townes, *Womanist Ethics and the Cultural Production of Evil* (New York: Palgrave Macmillan, 2007).

13 Keeanga Yamahtta-Taylor, "Martin Luther King's Radical Anti-capitalism," *The Paris Review*, January 15, 2018, https://www.theparisreview.org/blog/2018/01/15/remembering-martin-luther-kings-radical-class-politics/.

14 Transport Workers Union of America, Address by Dr. Martin Luther King Jr. TWU's 11th Constitutional Convention, 1961. https://www.twu.org/wp-content/uploads/2021/02/MLK_ConventionSpeech.pdf. Accessed on October 1, 2023.

15 Martin Luther King Jr., *Strength to Love* (Minneapolis: Fortress Press, 1963).

16 Brandon Terry and Shatema Threadcraft, "Gender Trouble: Manhood, Inclusion, and Justice," in *To Shape A New World: Essays on the Political Philosophy of Martin Luther King, Jr.*, eds. Tommie Shelby and Brandon M. Terry (Cambridge, MA: The Belknap Press of Harvard University Press, 2018), 210.

17 Martin Luther King, "I Have a Dream," University of Minnesota Human Rights Library, August 28, 1963, Retrieved from: http://hrlibrary.umn.edu/education/lutherspeech.html.

18 Delores Williams, *Sisters in the Wilderness: The Challenge of Womanist God-Talk* (Maryknoll, NY: Orbis Books, 1993), 146–148.

19 Delores Williams, *Sisters in the Wilderness*, 148.

20 Karl Barth, *The Doctrine of Reconciliation*, vol. 4, part 2 of *Church Dogmatics* (London: Bloomsbury Publishing, 1956), 180.

CHAPTER 5

1 For more on the life of Rev. Addie Wyatt, see Marcia Walker-McWilliams, *Reverend Addie Wyatt: Faith and the Fight for Labor, Gender, and Racial Equality* (Champaign: University of Illinois Press, 2016).

2 Marcia Walker-McWilliams, *Reverend Addie Wyatt*, 106.

3 Marcia Walker-McWilliams, *Reverend Addie Wyatt*, 107.

4 "Rev. Addie Wyatt," interview by Joan McGann Morris, Working Women's History Project, https://wwhpchicago.org/the-reverend-addie-l.-wyatt.html.

5 "(1977) The Combahee River Collective Statement," Black Past, https://www.blackpast.org/african-american-history/combahee-river-collective-statement-1977/.

6 "(1977) The Combahee River Collective Statement," Black Past.

7 Charles Marsh, *The Beloved Community: How Faith Shapes Social Justice Form the Civil Rights Movement to Today* (New York: Basic Books, 2005), 89.

CHAPTER 6

1 "W. E. B. Du Bois (William Edward Burghardt), 1868–1963, Economic Co-operation among Negro Americans," Documenting the American South, https://docsouth.unc.edu/church/dubois07/dubois.html.

2 John S. Ahlquist, "Labor Unions, Political Representation, and Economic Inequality," Annual Review of Political Science 20:1 (2017), 409–432.

3 1 Timothy 5:18; Galatians 2:10.

4 James 5:1–6.

5 Ruth Wilson Gilmore, "Abolition Geography and the Problem of Innocence," in *Futures of Black Radicalism*, ed. Gaye Theresa Johnson and Alex Lubin (New York: Verso Books, 2017).

6 The Brookings Institute: the social insurance system in the US: policies to protect workers and families; see also University of Wisconsin-Madison: Institute for Research on Poverty, Social Insurance Programs.

7 Economic Policy Institute: Codetermination and Power in the Workplace.

8 Ewan McGaughey, *Democracy in America at Work: The History of Labor's Vote in Corporate Governance*, 42 Seattle U. L. Rev. 697 (2019).

9 Matthew Bodie and Grant Hayden, "Codetermination: The Missing Alternative in American Governance," *The Law and Political Economy Project*, January 13, 2022, https://lpeproject.org/blog/codetermination-the-missing-alternative-in-corporate-governance/.

10 Bodie and Hayden, "Codetermination."

11 Keri Day, "Feminist and Womanist Responses to Neoliberalism" (lecture, Yale University, New Haven, CT).

12 Allison P. Gise Johnson, "Fulfilling Katie's Deepest Desire," *Journal of Feminist Studies in Religion* 35, no. 1 (Spring 2019): 107–108.

13 Martin Luther King Jr., *All Labor Has Dignity* (Boston: Beacon Press, 2012).

CHAPTER 7

1 Acts 17:6.

2 Karl Marx, "Theses on Feuerbach," Marxists.org, accessed November 8, 2023, https://www.marxists.org/archive/marx/works/1845/theses/.

3 Common, "Glory," Common and John Legend, track 1 on *Selma* soundtrack, Paramount Music, 2014.

4 Emilie Townes, *Womanist Ethics and the Cultural Production of Evil* (New York: Palgrave Macmillan, 2007).

5 Princeton Student Climate Initiative, Racial Disparities and Climate Change, https://psci.princeton.edu/tips/2020/8/15/racial-disparities-and-climate-change; International Monetary Fund, United States, At A Glance, 2023 https://www.imf.org/en/Countries/USA#ataglance.

6 Milton Friedman, *Capitalism and Freedom* (Chicago: University of Chicago Press, 1962).

7 "Economic, social, and cultural rights," United Nations Human Rights, https://www.ohchr.org/en/human-rights/economic-social-cultural-rights.

8 Angela Bronner Helm, "Black Women Now the Most Educated Group in US," *The Root,* June 5, 2016, https://www.theroot.com/black-women-now-the-most-educated-group-in-us-1790855540; and "Equal Pay for African American Women," National Women's Law Center, August 16, 2016, https://nwlc.org/resource/equal-pay-for-african-american-women/.

9 See W. E. B. Du Bois, *Black Reconstruction in America, 1860–1880* (New York: Harcourt, Brace, 1935).

10 Institute of Policy Studies, Kairos Center for Religions, Rights, and Social Justice. *The Souls of Poor Folk: Auditing America 50 years after the poor People's Campaign challenged racism, poverty, the economy, militarism, and our national morality,* April 2018.

11 Keri Day, "Feminist and Womanist Responses to Neoliberalism" (lecture, Yale University, New Haven, CT).

12 Rep. Pramila Jayapal, D, (WA-07), press release co-issued with the National Domestic Workers Alliance, "*Jayapal, Gillibrand, and Luján Re-Introduce National Domestic Workers Bill of Rights Alongside National Domestic Workers Alliance,*" https://jayapal.house.gov/2021/07/29/domestic-workers-bill-of-rights/.

13 Ephesians 4:25, NRSV.

14 Osita Nwanevu, "Spreading the Gospel of Modern Monetary Theory," *New Republic*, October 3, 2019; also see, Stephanie Kelton, *The Deficit Myth: Modern Monetary Theory and the Birth of the People's Economy* (New York: Public Affairs, 2020).

15 David Danelski, "Poverty is the 4th greatest cause of U.S. deaths," UC Riverside, News, https://news.ucr.edu/articles/2023/04/17/poverty-4th-greatest-cause-us-deaths.

16 John 16:33, NIV.

17 Jamye Wooten. "Interlocking Principles," Cllctivly, https://cllctivly.org/about/.

18 Delores Williams, "The Color of Feminism: Or Speaking the Black Woman's Tongue," *Journal of Religious Thought* 43, no. 1 (1986).

EPILOGUE

1 Howard Thurman, *Deep Is the Hunger: Meditations for Apostles of Sensitiveness*, Meditation 5 (Richmond, IN: Friends United Press, 1978).

2 Thurman, *Deep Is the Hunger.*

3 Howard Thurman, *Mysticism and Social Action: Lawrence Lectures and Discussions with Dr. Howard Thurman* (London: International Association for Religious Freedom, 2015).

4 Psalm 19:1, NIV.